There's no place like home

Martin Coffey, B.A. (Hons)

Front cover: Martin Coffey, First Holy Communion Day 1958

Dedication

I dedicate this book to my seven brothers and seven sisters: Vera, Chrissie, Billy, Bernard, Noel, Paddy, Brendan, Anne, Mary, Catherine, Tony, June, Helen and Joseph.

"No man ever steps into the same river twice"

Heraclitus of Ephesus

(c. 535 – c. 475 BC)

Prologue

In recent times I have taken to writing more stories of what I can remember of the life and times of my family growing up in the suburbs of North Dublin. I also began writing stories that I had heard from my parents, who both grew up in one of the poorer areas of the City. Some of the stories my mother told me are written in poetic form to help emphasis the tragedy of some of those young children that she had known.

Growing up as the middle child in a family of fifteen children, eight boys and seven girls, was a relatively easy task for me. With seven younger and seven older sibling I was cushioned in the middle. We all had a role to play in the home, some more so than others and thankfully we all survived to adulthood in one piece. We were no different to the vast majority of families living in Dublin from the 1940's to the 1960's. I never knew any rich families but I certainly was aware of many poor ones. Poverty is no respecter of persons and once a family fell into its clutches there was little or no hope of escape. Most families in those early years just about kept their heads above water.

Our parents and grandparents were indeed great people, they did the best they could with what little they had. My childhood was full of innocence. I knew nothing of the terrible stress that my parents were under in their attempt to provide for us. My dinner was always on the table when I arrived home from school, I was given my Tea at six o'clock and I went to Mass every Sunday. That was my basic routine, week in, week out. In between, I was out playing with my friends or off on some adventure with my brother. I had no understanding of death, I knew that babies were found under a head of cabbage, I was aware of, but unsure, about the dangers from *"Strange Men"*, especially those who sat beside me in the darkness of the Picture House and I knew that if I kissed a dead person they would never come back to haunt me. In general, I never felt unsafe, because I was forever surrounded by a large family and an even larger group of young pals.

In setting out to write this book, I wanted to record, for future generations, what life in general was like for many young boys and girls growing up in Dublin before the introduction of the EEC/Common Market/EU days. To write of a time when Ireland enjoyed life without the interference of Political Correctness, a time when we as children were allowed to be innocent and carefree. I would also like to record some of the hardships endured by my parents, an older generation, who struggled on a daily basis to feed their ever-growing family.

This book is laid out in stories and not in chapters and because of this, I have decided not to include a *"Contents Page"*.

I hope that you enjoy what you are about to read.

Story One

Martin Coffey 1952

We were all the same

1) Growing up at home I had seven brothers and seven sisters, so nothing was ever my own.

2) I never slept in a bed on my own, unless I was sick and that was only during the day time.

3) I never wore bijamers (pyjamas) to bed because I never knew what they were. I always kept my shirt and stockin's on in bed. When I say mine, they probably belonged to one of my older brothers.

4) I never wore underpants, never knew such a thing existed. Most of the girls around where I lived never wore anything like that either.

5) My mother brought me to school on my first day. After that it was up to one of my older brothers to bring me but on most occasions, I made my own way to school with one of my little pals, it was almost a half a mile away from where I lived. I remember my mother had to cut the tail off my little shirt because it was too long and sticking out the end of my trousers. I have great memories of my school days.

6) The only time I can remember ever getting new clothes was for my First Holy Communion and my Confirmation. My mother would have to pawn them afterwards to pay the money back to the Loan Society or the money lender.

7) Any new second-hand clothes or shoes that I got came from the Ivy Market. There was a Dealer there that my mother knew from years ago and she'd always put things to one side in case my mother called in. Then there was the stuff in the great big cardboard boxes that my older sister sent home from the hospital she nursed in, in England. I remember wearing an English School Blazer out of that box and all my pals thought I was posh. And of course, there was always the relations, the cousins and that, who had grown out of their clothes. My Aunt Kathleen gave my older sister a jumper that was too tight on her and when it became too tight for my sister my older brother wore it.

8) Whatever food was put in front of me at the dinner table, I had to eat it, otherwise someone else would and that was it, I'd have to go hungry for the rest of the day.

9) Most of us had to stand around our table whenever we had our dinner or tea because we only had four chairs and two of them were for my father and mother.

10) In our house the worse punishment of all was being sent up to bed early and especially in the middle of the day when all my pals would be playing outside.

11) Every Saturday morning, I was roped in with the rest of our gang to clean the house. My mother was in charge and would give us all some job or other to do. The skirting-boards had to be cleaned and dusted, the brass number on our hall door and the keyhole had to be polished with Brasso, the windows had to be washed, under our beds had to be swept, the fireplace had to be cleaned out, the big kitchen table had to be scrubbed and polished, the kitchen sink and the Gas Stove cleaned down, all the floors had to be washed and newspaper put down on them until they were dry, all the bed sheets had to be changed and DDT shaken over the clean ones when they were put on the beds, that was to kill all the Hoppers. We had Hoppers in the bed and Fleas in our head. The Hoppers lived under the rim at the edge of our mattress and some Saturday mornings, if myself and the brother had nothing else to do, we'd turn up the edge of the rim and start killing off all the Hoppers by squeezing them between our thumb nails, there were literally hundreds of them, and they'd be swollen with the blood that they had sucked out of us during the previous night. When we'd squash them, the blood would squirt up into our faces, it was a great laugh altogether.

Every now and then my mother would get out her *"Fine Comb"* and we'd all be lined up from youngest to eldest to have our heads searched for fleas, or Lice as they're called today. I would kneel down on the floor in front of my mother and put my head down on the newspaper on her lap and away she'd go. I remember one of the sister's roaring and screaming that she didn't want it done to her lovely long hair, so the Ma' ups and cuts her hair short, you could hear a pin drop, my sister never complained again.

12) Every Saturday night we all had to be washed, some of us, like me for instance, were washed in the kitchen sink, while the older ones went upstairs to the bath and there was always at least three of them in it at the same time. My father would be running up and down our stairs with buckets of hot water. On a Sunday morning in the summer, our sandals, that my older sister sent home from England, had to be white-washed and put out on the kitchen window ledge to dry in the sun. I only ever got a clean shirt of a

Sunday and I wouldn't take that off until the next Sunday. It would have loads of blood spots on the collar from the Hoppers who'd be sucking the blood out of my neck while I was asleep.

Home-Made Slingshots or Gats

13) We always went out to Dollymount for our holidays but only one day at a time. The very odd occasion we would be brought out to Portmarnock, to the swimming bathes in Blackrock or to Bray with all the Tenants Association people on the bus. There would be a great sing-song with all the children and the Mammy's on the way out and on the way home some Oul Fella, with a few drinks taken, would start off singing Irish Rebel songs and we'd all fall asleep because we'd be bunched from running and playing on the beach and in the water all day long and most of us would be burnt to a crisp from the Sun.

14) We never gave cheek to an adult or a neighbour, that was punishable by firing-squad because you'd get a box from the neighbour and then if the Ma' got to hear about it she'd give it to you double time and then when the Da' came in from work and heard what you'd done you'd get a triple clout. Respect for our elders was something that was drummed into us from a very early age.

15) In the summer months, on our school holidays, we were allowed to play out until about ten o'clock at night. In the winter and of a school time, we were in bed by nine o'clock. When I started work at fifteen and was wearing Longers I was allowed to stay up a little bit later. The Da' was always the last one to go to bed. He'd make sure we were all in and then he'd lock the front and back doors.

Old coins from the 1940's-1960's

16) The Ma' and Da' always slept in the same room as the girls, usually the front bedroom because it was the biggest room. Us boys slept in the back bedroom that probably measured about ten feet by eight feet. We had three beds in that room and a wardrobe, I don't know why we had that because we had nothing to hang up in it. The eldest brother always had a bed to himself because he smoked. That left three of us younger ones in each of the other two beds. We were never allowed into the front parlour, as the Ma' called it, that was for visitors only, so it was rarely used.

17) We were always sent off to the Picture House after our dinner of a Sunday. When I was working, I use to go of a Saturday or

Sunday night with my pals, that is until I started *"Mottin"* and then the pals never got a look in. Some Sunday's the Da' would take us up along the canal picking Blackberries and the Ma' would always make loads of jam with them.

18) My younger sisters were always great at playing games with their pals, skipping with two ropes, running along the road skipping on their own or with a pal, playing shop with broken pieces of delph they called *"Chainey"* for money, playing at doctor's and nurse's with their dolls and prams, gangs of them playing Piggy Beds or Hop-Scotch, swinging on a rope tied up around a lamp-post, Queenie Eye Oh, Red Rover-Red Rover, Hide and seek was usually played late in the evening just before dark, Postman's Knock, chasing after each other playing *"You're on it"* and sometimes the girls would sit around in a group and start singing songs they had learned in school or ones that they had heard on the Wireless. The Hoola Hoop was another great game the girls would play. My little sister Anne always had a great big bow in her hair, right on the top of her head and loads of her pals had as well. My two older sisters went out to work at 13 and 14 years of age, they bought themselves a bicycle each on Hire Purchase, there was no cross-bar on them because they were girl's bikes.

19) The boy's all-time favourite game was Cowboys and Indians and then there was football with a ball that was burst and about fifty lads running after it trying to score a goal, the goal posts were usually a couple of jumpers or coats belonging to some of the lads.

Then there was swimming up in the canal or maybe in the local open air swimming baths, was another great thing to do, fishing for Pinkeens, or going off with a bunch of lads to rob an orchard was always a great adventure, making money by collecting old newspapers and empty bottles that we brought to what we now call the recycle man.

We played a game called *"The Moul"* whereby you opened up one of the small *"Uisce"* shores outside your gate and you'd toss a penny or a ha'penny into it, playing marbles with a *"Scrunchie"*, running along with a hoop and a stick was a great thing to do as well because you could out-run all of your pals you'd be going so quick. Then there was Conkers with chestnuts from the trees in the Phoenix Park. There were no limits to where our imaginations could go because we had the freedom to come and go as we pleased as long as we didn't get into trouble. I know our local playground was a great place to spend time, up on the swings or the Monkey-Puzzle, we'd stay there all day after school. I suppose the place to go for a really big adventure for me was up to the nearby Phoenix Park.

We'd always make for the Azoo and we had to walk around outside peeking in at the animals because we didn't have the money to pay in, it was far too dear then and still is today, in my opinion. And then we went to Sodality of a Friday night and Sunday morning at ten o'clock. We told lies to the priest in the Confession Box of a Saturday, you would let your pal hit you on the top of the head with a stick to see if it hurt and you had to do the same to him, having a pull on someone's cigarette and hope the Da' didn't hear about it and so much more.

20) If there's one thing we never were back in those days it was *"Bored"*, we didn't know the meaning of the word. There was always something to do or to be done or some place to go. In our Parish there was a great Variety Club that always put on musical shows in the school hall, there were accordion clubs for both boys and girls, running clubs, hurling clubs, football clubs, clubs in the Playground, record clubs for music lovers, photo clubs, knitting and sewing clubs, no matter what your interest was someone had a Club for it.

21) But I suppose the most important thing that I had growing up in the 1950's and 1960's was the guiding hand of my parents, always checking and watching that I kept out of trouble, a word of warning here and there to keep me on the straight and narrow and the odd kick in the pants when I deserved it.

22) We were forever reminded to never bring the Garda to our door, what would the neighbours think? We were sent to weekly Mass and Confession and we had a picture up in our hallway of the Pope and a Holy Water font to bless ourselves with every time we were going outside or going up to bed at night. The Da' singing in the toilet as he shaved of a Sunday morning, the Ma' at her Singer sewing machine making dresses for my sisters and all the ironing that had to be done on a Friday night as she listened to some story or other on the wireless. These were some of the elements that glued our family together through thick and thin, tough times no doubt. For me, they were very happy times, times that I would not change for all the tea in China.

23) This was a time when it was almost a Mortal Sin not to have a job when you left school. There was no such thing as staying in bed all day and lazing about the house. We were told, in no uncertain terms, to get out there and get a job, it didn't matter what it was, you took whatever was offered. Similar to my father, some of my siblings left school at 13/14 years of age and started work straightaway and never stopped until retirement age. And that's how it was for everybody, no exceptions. In our house, if you didn't have a job then you were basically sent to the end of the dinner queue until you had.

THE SCHOOL TEACHER

The Broadway Cinema Manor Street

My older brothers and sister went to the Pictures here,
sometimes they paid in with large Jam Jars.

Story Two

**L-R: Hughie Quinn with Brendan and Paddy Coffey and
behind the hedge, Martin Coffey, 1952**

A Working-Class Family

Sometime after the founding of the Irish Free State, the Lord Mayor
of Dublin, Ald. Alfie Byrne raised questions with the newly
appointed government regarding the housing difficulties of the
workers and the poor of Dublin and in particular, those families
who were living in derelict tenements houses and side streets of

dilapidated cottages and houses. The Dublin Master Builders Association stated that the shortage of materials and skilled labour would have to be surmounted if the output of housing was to be increased. Soon after however, a government programme of house building began in earnest. My mother told me that when she applied for a house, each family had to have at least three children in order to qualify.

Most all of the houses in our area were built off the same plan, two bedrooms and a toilet upstairs with a kitchen and parlour downstairs, they were known as a *"Parlour House"*. Other houses had three bedrooms upstairs and their toilet was downstairs, out by the back door. It didn't seem to matter how many children a family had where bedrooms were concerned; it was just the luck of the draw which one your family was allocated. Each house had a front and back garden.

I don't think we ever really looked on ourselves as a working-class family. The people in our neighbourhood never had the time to give themselves a label like that and especially those who had no work to go to. A lot of people raised chickens in their back gardens and I remember one neighbour who even had a goat. They let it sleep upstairs with the children. Another family kept a monkey in their attic. Some people used the parlour as a third bedroom. We didn't, because our parlour was kept for visitors to sit in. The door was usually kept locked and the room was rarely used. Most visitor that came to our house were related to us so they were brought straight into our kitchen, where the kettle was constantly on the boil and a cup of tea ready to hand.

One neighbour in particular, slept in her parlour beside the window. She sold broken seaside rock to the children in the neighbourhood. She kept the rock under her horse-hair mattress and would pull out a handful in exchange for a penny any time a child knocked on her window. She spent most of her time in the bed. This is almost beyond belief because every bed in the area was alive and walking with fleas and all sorts of smells and God only knows what else. In a lot of cases it really didn't matter whose child you were or to what house you belonged, because when the need arose, most everyone helped out.

Other families in the area had even less than we had. We were lucky in that our father had a permanent job. Many men in the area were unemployed and there were some who were even unemployable. Those who could, took the boat to England and looked for work there. Some men even started up a second family over there. A very odd time money would somehow find its way home to the first family.

Once in a while some of the men would even return home for a holiday but would always go back to their second family. It was never mentioned of course that the parents had separated or split up. It was always said that he was *"Working across the water"*. We had a neighbour who worked for the summer months in England selling ice cream and then he'd return home to Dublin for the winter and go around selling coal door to door.

Brendan and Anne Coffey

You could always tell the women whose husbands were absent from the home. Early in the mornings, possibly from around six or seven o'clock, you could see some of these women cleaning their windows or sweeping down the pathway outside of their houses. Some of them even went so far as to sweep the roadway outside their house. They would spend hours rubbing and polishing the brasses on their front door. They always had a smell of carbolic soap and disinfectant. In later years I asked my mother why they did these sorts of things and it was then that I discovered about the husband in England. These women always wore their aprons under their coats and had their headscarves knotted tightly under their chins. Their noses were blue from the cold and their fingers were frozen to the bone. They never seemed to smile.

Maybe it was because they felt they had nothing to smile about. Perhaps the second wife was doing enough smiling for the both of them. Other families didn't give any attention to their homes or children. I suppose mentally they had never moved out of the derelict tenement buildings where they had come from. There were a few families who lived in total denial of their circumstances, afraid to admit that they had fallen on hard times and too proud to look for help from a neighbour. They considered themselves a cut above everyone else. They would go into city centre to borrow from the moneylenders. They wouldn't want people to know their business.

Some boys in my school would collect any bread that other boys had thrown away and bring it home to their family. One boy told me that his mother would make bread pudding with it for their dinner. There were some areas of terrible poverty. Incest between father and daughter was not too uncommon in some families. One girl I know of had her father and brothers visit her bed on a nightly basis. When she began working in a sewing factory at 14 years of age, she mentioned it to some of her friends in passing. The girls were horrified and told her to stop it and to tell her mother about it. When she arrived home, she told her mother what her friends in work had said. Her mother set about beating her and refused to let her go back to work.

We didn't have very much in our house. Everything was very basic, nothing fancy or uppity and rarely if ever did we have anything that was new. There was a blue and white kitchen dresser that stood against the wall next to the kitchen door. My mother kept a metal bread-bin in the bottom part of it. The bread-bin, as far as I know, was a present that my parents had received on their wedding day so very long ago. We had some small egg spoons known as the Twelve Apostles that they also received as a wedding present. One of the drawers in the Dresser had a collection of knives and forks and other odd bits of cutlery. And of course, my mother always had to have a *"Button Drawer"*, where she kept spare zips for dresses or jackets, buttons for shirts, trousers and coats and many more such things that she considered would come in handy someday. I remember the drawers had a distinct smell, not a fragrance, just a smell.

On the wall beside the dresser was the one and only electrical outlet in the entire house, a double socket. My father had it jammed tight with all sorts of double adaptors and plugs that had electric leads stretched in all directions. There were no electric sockets upstairs or in the hallway. Everything electrical started and finished from that one point in the kitchen. We had a table and very few chairs but certainly not enough to seat us all at the one time. My father made a long stool from some scraps of timber he had. Most of us had to stand at the table when eating our meals. My father and mother sat at the head of the table, my father on the right-hand side and my mother beside him.

We were more or less placed around the table in order of our ages. The eldest sat nearer to our parents and the smaller ones stood around the rest of the table. If there were any other chairs or stools it was usually the smallest ones who were given them, as they couldn't reach up to the table too well. The boys in our house all slept in the one room, usually the back bedroom. This room only measured about ten feet by eight feet. There were five or six of us in this room at any one time. I remember a time when there were three beds, a wardrobe and a baby's cot in the room. Every night the windows and bedroom door were shut tight to keep out the cold. Any fresh air was soon replaced with the smell of dirty socks, farts, belching, coughing and cigarette smoke. My parents slept in the front room with the girls and whatever baby was around at the time.

In later years and after my father had died, my mother loved her nights out at the bingo. She said that it was more for the company and laugh that she went for. There was a group of women that she was friends with and they all met up at the bingo. Sometimes she would hear a good joke and she would try to remember it for my Dad. On her way home she would suddenly realise that he was not at home anymore. She would then sit up in bed and tell the joke to him anyway. She would often cry herself to sleep afterwards.

Story Three

Furniture for Sale

I'm not too sure where my Uncle Paddy took this photograph but it certainly says a lot about the time it was taken, probably sometime around the 1940's. I know that when my parents were first married in the 1930's and had moved into a room above a Butcher's Shop in Parnell Street, it was of a Saturday morning and the room was empty except for an old Messenger Bike with the front wheel missing off it.

They had nothing when they first moved in, no furniture of any description, no net curtains, nothing. My mother's older brother Johnnie and his pal arrived up with a second-hand single mattress for them and a Bolster (that's a long pillow) that was full of stains from people dribbling on it while they slept. He probably got them down the Hill in Cumberland Street. But as my mother said, it was something to start off with. In later years they had one of them great big wooden framed beds like the big one in the photograph that's leaning up against the shop window. My mother said it came with a handle to wind the springs tight with, at one end there were two big bolts that were tightened whenever the springs sagged in the middle, as most beds used to do then and that's how it was fixed.

Now, my mother said that their room was a step-up from the tenement house because it had an indoor toilet downstairs where the Butcher used to go when he needed to. She said that he had a shed out at the back of the shop where he would slaughter some of the animals that he sold. Their room looked out onto the street below and my mother loved to stand looking out at the world going by, she was 18 years old and all grown up.

Some of the second-hand furniture didn't come cheap and especially if it was in good condition. Take the big bed with the spring on it, now if that didn't come with a winding handle then it was cheaper than if it had a handle. Over time and eventually, my mother and father got all their bits and pieces together, including a fire-grate and a poker. My parents used to sit in of an evening and he'd be telling her all about his years away with the British Army and what it was like to shoot a real rifle for the first time and how it was not one they used to see in the cowboy films in the Elec picture house in Talbot Street. She'd sometimes fall asleep while he was still talking away into the night.

Despite how little they had they both seemed to be contented with their own room. My father was finding it hard to get any work, things were hard back then and nothing ever came easy. The Ma' had an uncle who had a friend who worked for a tea company in Liffey Street and sometimes the uncle would drop up to see her with a pocketful of tea, although my mother said it was more sawdust than tea but none the less, she was grateful to her uncle for thinking of them.

My father's uncle, Sonny Doyle from Railway Street arrived up one night with a long wooden stool that he had made for them so that they could sit together at the fire. Another time, according to my mother, two of my father's cousins called by in the middle of the night with a lovely set of delph and a tea pot that they had *"Found"* somewhere or other and thought that my parents might like to have them. Up to then they drank out of jam jars and the water for the tea was boiled in a Billy Can over the fire and that's where my mother did all her cooking as well, over the fire.

Now, it wasn't too long after that when their first baby arrived, so my mother and baby girl moved in with granny for a few weeks until Mammy was back on her feet again. The new baby was so tiny that my granny made a little bed for her in a drawer in the sideboard in her flat in Cumberland Street. It was around this time that my father was given holiday work on the buses working out of Clontarf Garage. And so, it seemed that things were looking up for them now. The Da' managed to stay working on the buses for a little longer than expected, he had probably told one of the bosses about the new baby arriving. This was a time before official Bus Stops. My father said that the bus drivers would race one another along the seafront of Clontarf to see who would get the first passenger. People would stand at any point along the edge of the footpath and put their hand out to stop the bus.

With the extra money coming in they were able to go out and buy a few more pieces of second-hand furniture and my mother said she was thrilled when my father and her brother Johnnie brought home a kitchen table, *"Imagine that..."*, she said to me, *"...having your own kitchen table"*. And her mother's best pal gave them a bucket so that they wouldn't have to go down the dark stairs at night to use the toilet.

It was a few years on when my father was given a temporary job as a Bank Porter in the Bank of Ireland on College Green. This was thanks to one of the leaders of the then Belvedere Newsboys' Club that my father had joined at twelve years of age. The first thing that the Bank gave him was a note to go to a tailor's and get a suit made, he had to wear that and his collar and tie to work every day. Eventually he was taken on fulltime. My mother said that he always looked so smart and proud going out to work in the mornings and he all dolled up and cleaned and shaved. And herself with another baby on the way, happy days.

The games we played

Story Four

Stillorgan 1942

In 1942 my father was having a hard time trying to find a day's work. My parents were then living with their three young children in a tenement room on Summerhill. A neighbour asked my father if he wanted a few months' work. They both went to the Labour Exchange in Gardiner Street where your man told the Supervisor that he didn't want this job and that my father could have it instead.

The job entailed digging ditches to facilitate pipe laying in Stillorgan in South County Dublin. So, for the first three weeks my father walked from Summerhill to Stillorgan, did his days digging and walked home again. My older sister remembered that some days my mother would walk with the three children and the pram to

Stillorgan with a bit of dinner for him. My father and several other men, were given some space in a garden allotment in nearby Punchestown. He would spend some time after work and his half day on Saturday, in the allotment.

After three weeks my father' bought a second-hand bicycle and cycled to work and home each day. He used to give one of his old school pals, who was also employed on the roads in Stillorgan, a lift on the crossbar of the bike. They both took turns on the crossbar and my father said they'd spend most of the time singing songs they'd learned from their days in the British Army.

My father, like a lot of father's back then, thought nothing of travelling that distance for a day's work. They were great men who put their family first above all else. And of course, they wore whatever shoes or boots they had on their feet, there was no such thing in their world as Runners or Sneakers when they took off walking. The men in this photograph who are wearing overalls are the Tradesmen. Others, like my father, wore whatever clothes they normally wore, waistcoats and all.

Story Five

My parents in Talbot Street

This photo of my parents was taken in Talbot Street in the early 1950's. They were married in 1938. In 1941 they had three young children. Work was very scarce back then and my father found it very hard to get work. They had so little money to live on that my father approached his Parish Priest for a letter for help from the Saint Vincent de Paul. The priest told him that he would call around to see his tenement room and assess his needs. My father rushed home and told my mother that the Parish Priest was calling. She tidied up their room for his visit. When he saw the place so clean and tidy, he told my father that he didn't think they were in need and walked out.

My father ran after the priest for an explanation but the oul priest refused to speak to him. My father told the priest that he would go to the Protestants for help. Within an hour two men from the *"Vincent's"* called to see my parents and gave them some kind of help. My mother told me that she was fuming at my father for going to the Parish Priest in the first place, she said she'd rather starve than go begging to the priest, she was a fierce independent woman.

The coat my mother is wearing in this photograph was second-hand, my mother added a piece onto the bottom of the coat so that it would fit her. The photo was taken by a street photographer. They were on their way to visit my father's youngest sister and her family in her flat in Sheriff Street. I remember one time in particular when a priest came to our house collecting his Easter Dues. He never looked at or spoke to my mother. He only addressed my father before putting his hand out for money.

At that time my parents had at least ten children and could ill afford to be giving money away. The priest stood with his back to my mother while he spoke to my father. My mother had no time for the clergy. She refused to be *"Churched"* after having a baby when my father told her that the priest said it was a sin to get pregnant and he should tell it in Confession. She told me she was fuming over that.

Like so many other parents, mine had it very tough in their early years of marriage. Always making and mending, never throwing anything out, hand-me-down clothes and shoes were the norm. Reaching out and helping neighbours who were less well off than themselves. We'd sometimes wake up in the morning to find a neighbour's child sleeping in beside us, their poor mother might have been taken into hospital during the night. And that's the way it was back then, nobody looking for medals or praise, for helping out when the need arose.

The Old Workhorse

Story Six

The Da' and Ma'

My mother worked hard all her life, from the age of 14, when she started off in a Rosary Bead Factory in town, right up to the day she died. It was only in her later years that she had it easier than most of the previous years of her life. In between, I don't think she ever got a moment to herself, raising fifteen children, looking after my father and keeping the house going. Now, my father too worked hard all his life, starting off at ten years of age selling newspapers around some of the pubs in town. In later years he joined the British Army as a way of keeping out of trouble and to be able to give money to his aunt, May Doyle, who reared him. My mother told me that she had a very happy childhood despite the poverty and squalor of the area where she lived.

She didn't see anything wrong with that because it was the way everyone around her lived and nobody was any different to anyone else. Like her own mother before her, she always looked for the good in people and had a great respect for her elders. She said that back then you were never allowed to give cheek to an adult and if you did, they could give you a box in the ear and if your mother heard about it then you'd get another one off her as well.

I know the biggest threat that my mother could make to us if we misbehaved was that she was going to tell the Da' when he came in from work. We'd be dreading him coming in through the house with his bicycle in case she said anything to him but in most cases the threat was enough.

After they were married, they lived in many different flats around town, depending on the rent and always hoping to get a tenement room down near the hall door so she wouldn't have to haul a pram and half a dozen little ones up and down the stairs several times a day. In some of the flats, like the one over the Butcher's shop in Parnell Street where they lived for three months, they had water inside, whereas in the tenement house she didn't have water, electricity or a toilet indoors. They kept a bucket in the corner of the room with a piece of wood on top of it and then at night it was put out onto the Landing.

This is known as "The Side Chapel" in the Pro Cathedral. It is where both of my parents were originally baptised and later married. Many generations of my extended family were also baptised and married here.

My mother said that when they moved to the two-bedroom house in Cabra it was like moving into Buckingham Palace with all the room and the indoor toilet and their own water tap. The bath wasn't installed until much later because of the war and that.

I remember I asked my mother did she and my father go off on honeymoon after they got married. Well, she certainly laughed at that. *"Will you go away outta that..."* she said *"...sure we barely had enough money to buy a loaf of bread without wasting money on a day trip to Bray"*. And that's how it was, no fancy wedding dress, no Hen Party in Spain, no Stag Party in Germany, just family and a few friends meeting up in the little side chapel in the Pro Cathedral for the ceremony and then off to work they both went. They met up with some people in the pub after work and then home to the Granny's flat for bacon and cabbage and a few more bottles. The next morning it was back to work and life went on.

For most of her married life my mother rarely had any clothes that were new. Like ourselves, nearly everything she wore was second-hand. Sometimes, she might cut up an old dress and make something of it for herself or my older sisters. There were plenty of places back then where she could go for second-hand clothes and shoes for herself and my father or for us.

As the older brothers and sister began their working lives things calmed down a bit with the extra money coming in. I remember my mother going into Guiney's for new Net Curtain material for our parlour window. She would make them up herself or maybe Granny O'Brien from next door would sew them up for her. You see, having your own parlour and net curtains meant the world to my mother and many other women who had lived in the tenements, it was a little step up the social ladder so to speak. Her first pair of net curtains were held up with a bit of twine because she had nothing else.

And every Saturday we'd all be hauled up like an army of ants to clean the house from top to bottom. She had an awful fear of any of us getting sick or getting Polio or that, because a lot of children from where she was born died young from TB. The skirting boards in every room had to be cleaned, the doors had to be scrubber down and the job I always got and hated the most was cleaning the brass door knocker and key hole and there was a little brass wheel in under the weatherboard at the bottom of our hall door that had to be cleaned and polished as well. Now, I used to wonder who would ever see that little wheel, but my mother insisted that it had to be polished.

Most of us older ones left home and went to England to live, some short term and some for a life time. And that tended to make things easier all round at home. I remember when my father came home and announced that we were getting two sets of bunk beds delivered in a couple of days, we couldn't believe it, we were rich at last. I didn't have to sleep in the same bed with my two brothers now I was eighteen, I was getting a bunk bed all to myself. I remember a couple of years after the 15th baby arrived in our house, my mother wanted to adopt a baby or to even foster one but she was turned down and that broke her heart I can tell you.

Gradually and over time things became much more manageable for my parents. Then my father retired from his job and my mother decided she was going out to find a job herself, and she did. She loved going out to work and being independent with her own few bob that she earned. She was able to buy herself a new dress and shoes, something that she would never have done years back but now she wanted to reward herself and rightly so.

My father sometimes worked two or three jobs a week for years to make sure there was enough money to pay the rent and put food on the table for all of us fifteen hungry mouths. Then came the time for him to say his final farewell to us and our mother, she was devastated and heartbroken. She managed day by day until her time too came to join him and leave all of us fifteen little chicks to fend for ourselves. I can tell you here and now that there's never a day goes by but we don't think of one or both of them and in any conversation I have with any of my sibling we always bring the Ma' and Da' into the story.

I remember when he used to head out on his bicycle at seven o'clock on a Sunday morning to Bray in County Wicklow. He would put in a day's work in a shop on the seafront rented by one of the Bank's customers from Camden Street. When he would finally arrive in Bray, he'd head straight to Mass first before starting off his days' work. He would eventually arrive home later that night at about eight or nine o'clock, worn out and hungry.

Story Seven

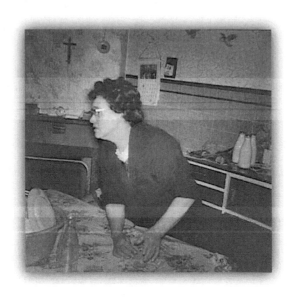

The Slippers

I always remember lying in bed and listening to the late-night sounds of our house. With so many children in our family, fifteen at the last count, late at night was the only time our house was ever quiet. I slept at the foot of the bed with my two brothers sleeping at the top, up near the bedroom window. Sometimes, a neighbour's little fella might be in beside me because his mother was poorly or gone into hospital. My eldest brother had a bed all to himself and he'd be sitting up with the light off, smoking his fag. I could hear him breathing every time he took a puff on the cigarette; the whole room would light up red from the glow of the ash. It was almost like a Lighthouse out on the edge of the sea warning the ships to keep away from the rocks.

In the other bed the rest of my brothers slept, three of them, all snoring, farting and breathing in harmony with each other, letting out the odd grunt and groan as they turned over from one side to the other. Sometimes, through the wall, I'd hear one of my younger sister's in the bigger bedroom, letting out a cry and calling for the Ma'. Then, just as before, everything would calm down and be as quiet as ever. The odd time I would hear our next-door neighbour flushing their toilet or banging their bedroom door as they headed off into the Twilights Zone. Far off in the distance I'd hear some oul dog howling and I knew that was a sign that someone was going to die.

My father and mother were always the last to come up the stairs to bed. They'd wait until everyone of us was safely home from Town or the Pictures and if they were unsure if we were all home or not, the Da' would go upstairs and have a head count. These were the days when anyone who went into town for some entertainment or other, would arrive home on the last bus, which always left town at half past eleven, on the blow of the Bus Inspector's whistle in O'Connell Street. You'd see young couples gum sucking the last kiss out of each other and then galloping the length of the street before jumping onto their bus and home they'd go. God forbid should any of us miss that bus and have to walk all the way home from town at that late hour and the Da' sitting up waiting for you to come in, you'd get a right telling off I can tell you. But that was a rare thing to happen because we all tried to be home on time.

Barney Doyle from Railway Street

I remember one time I was in a Dance Hall in Mountjoy Square with my older brother and I asked this Young One could I leave her home. I didn't realise that she lived in Ballyfermot, miles away out in the country on the far side of the Liffey, well that's what the brother told me when he heard what I had done, I thought she might have lived in Cabra. Anyway, he made me tell the Young One that we'd be back in a minute and off we ran for our bus home. I'd forgotten what he'd told me before about always asking where they lived first, I hope she's not still waiting for me to come back.

I'll never forget how it was in the quiet of the late night when I would hear the shuffle of my mother's slippered feet as she began to climb the stairs to bed. She told me in recent years, that she was so tired and worn out after a day of looking after all of us, she hadn't got the strength to lift her two feet off the floor, all she could do was shuffle her feet along. She was always up first in the mornings to put the kettle on for the Da's cuppa before he headed out on his bicycle to work.

The poor oul Ma' was worn out from getting us all out to school and work, making our beds, cleaning the kitchen, washing clothes, making sure the Da's shirt was ironed for work, shopping, getting our dinner ready, lighting the fire, helping the old neighbour from next door, hanging up her Net Curtains, feeding us all when we came in from school, usually one by one, having a dinner on the table for the Da', sewing buttons on a blouse, kissing the younger sister's knee better from when she fell and of course, trying to make sure she fed herself. She used to tell us that she had eyes in the back of her head, and we believed her of course, this was her way of letting us know that she missed nothing of our antics going on behind her back. So, if the brother was of a frame of mind to shovel a spoonful of sugar into his mouth when the Ma' was standing over the sink peeling potatoes, he'd always think twice, just in case those eyes were looking at him.

Sometimes I would hear the Da' calling in our poor oul mongrel of a dog, he'd sleep in front of the dying embers of our fire. Then there was the noise of the Da' closing the bolt on our back door, first the top one and then the bottom. For some strange reason he'd open the hall door and walk out as far as our gate to make sure it was closed and he'd stand there puffing on his cigarette for at least ten minutes. I suppose he was taking in the night air and thinking over his day and then planning his routine for tomorrow. Then he'd come back in to the house and lock up the hall door. It was a kind of nightly ritual that he carried out. I suppose in some way, in his head, he was back in the Army out on patrol, making sure the barracks was in a lock-down position.

The last thing he would do every night before going up to bed was, he'd bless himself from our Holy Water font beside the hall door and up he'd come, almost as worn out and as weary as the Ma'. I always seemed to nod off when I'd hear him snoring. I can just picture it now, the Ma' and Da' snuggled up together, like two oul soup spoons in the kitchen drawer, with all their little chickens safely tucked up in bed. And that was it for another night, all present and correct. That's how it went in our house for many years, night after night, no house alarm, no CCTV cameras to protect us, just our oul dog sleeping by the fireplace. We all felt safe and secure in the love of our parents, we didn't need anything else.

Story Eight

Newcastle Co. Down

The Ma' in 1935

In 1935 my mother was sixteen years old and working in a Rosary Bead factory, in Waterford Street, Dublin. This factory was owned and run by the Mitchell family. One of their sons, Charles Mitchell, became the first newsreader on Irish Television. I remember whenever he came on our Telly to read the news out, my mother would turn up the volume and tell us all to keep quiet, because she wanted to hear what Mister Mitchell had to say. In unison, we would all tell her that his name was Charles Mitchell and with an insistent glare, my mother would tell us that *"It's Mister Mitchell"*. I guess old habits died hard for the Ma' but back then, disrespect for ones *"Elders or Betters"*, was almost tantamount to murder. That school of thought was certainly ingrained into us in our growing up years because we were taught by our parents to always address our neighbours and older adults as either Mister or Misses. Now, if you broke that golden rule, you were guilty of being disrespectful and that always came with a severe penalty. My mother would sometimes tell us of her mother's old neighbours who were known as *"Mister Pig's Feet"* or *"Misses Win the War"* and there was also *"Misses Who Am I To You"*. But no matter what they were known as, they were always addressed, out of respect, as Mister or Misses.

My mother's best friend was Chrissie Sutton. She told me that the two of them were almost inseparable as best pals and that they went everywhere together. Their boyfriends, who they met in the Rosary Bead Factory, were from Ringsend and they would always go out on dates together. On the 23rd June 1935, a bus trip was arranged for the factory workers. Their first stop across the border was in Warrenpoint in the North of Ireland. They all wore their best clothes on that special occasion, bought through a Club that was run in the factory by the employees themselves. My mother told me that each of the girls would pay so much into the Club, out of their wages, every Friday. Every week one of the girls would be handed a clothing voucher for Guiney's or one of the many clothing shops in Dublin. They would get a whole new outfit, including shoes and a hat, in exchange for the voucher. Some of the girls would leave their turn until Christmas week or Easter and then get a new outfit for that particular holiday season.

My mother brought home a little souvenir for her mother, from Newcastle in County Down. When my granny died the souvenir came back to my mother. She kept that memory safely tucked away for all these years, in her China Cabinet in our parlour. For me, this is a little snapshot from my mother's teenage life, when all those years ago, four young girls from the tenement area of Dublin, on the edge of womanhood and without a care in the world, went on a day trip across the border.

My mother was sixteen years old at this time of her life and had never been outside of Dublin City centre before. Up to then, the furthest point south that she had ever travelled, was when her mother would take her shopping to Thomas Street and Meath Street. Other times, her mother would take her for a walk, up through the country lanes of Drumcondra to pick Blackberries. The Cat and Cage pub in Drumcondra was where city limits met the countryside, this was as far out as a bus would go to from O'Connell Street in city centre. In 1939 when my father and grandfather went to visit a relation of theirs, who was a patient out in Portrane Mental Hospital, they had to take the bus to Drumcondra and then travel by pony and trap from there out to the hospital.

In more recent years, I was fortunate to have a tape-recorder and with a little pushing and pulling, I managed to convince my mother to allow me to record her telling me all about her early life growing up in Dublin. She told me that her first job was in the Rosary Bead factory at Five Bob a week. So, I'll let her tell it to you as she told it to me. *'I started work when I was just gone fourteen. Well it was work, but you know, it was something. When I went in first, I went in on the buttons, polishing buttons. You'd have to sort the different sizes; you know, the 45's, the 35's and the 20's. When they finished doing buttons after a few years, we went on to do crosses, crosses for the Rosary Beads. I had to polish them. When they'd be slack, Paddy O'Neill, he was in charge then, he said to me "Will you go into the Grinding Room", they all hated going in there because it was full of dust. I didn't care, I'd go to the Grinding Room. You see when the Crosses would be cut out, they might be too thick and you would have to grind them down to the size to go on the beads. I could do that, I could grind them down, I could polish them and I could cut them out. Because I used to, when he'd ask me anything, I'd say yes, I'll do it. They were all made out of cow's horns and the hoofs off their feet.*

Then sometimes, some of the things we do, for the middle of the beads, they'd have this little heart shaped thing or maybe it'd be a Shamrock shape, and it might be "Souvenir of Knock" or souvenir of something else and different things like that. Well they'd have to be polished and they'd have to be Gilded, the lettering would be Gilded. Then you had to polish them so that the Gilding would be only in the lettering because when it'd be done it'd be all over them. I could join the beads. You got that you could pick up things if you were willing to, you know. Sure, I was a few years out of work and I went back to try and get my sister Kathleen a job. Mister O'Neill told me he'd no work for her but he'd give me job.

Now, there used to be a little young fella across the road from us in Elliott Place (This street was generally known by people in the Monto area as *"Ellitt Place"* and there are still people, even to this day, who use that pronunciation). *He was only a baby in a go-cart as you called them that time, and I used to take him out for walks with my little sister Kathleen and my other pal, May Davis, we used to go for walks and rambles, you know. So, we said this day we were going over to the park in the Customs House. It was a lovely day and we decided instead of going there, we'd go out to the beach in Dollymount but we never told anybody. We had only a bottle of water with us and we'd this young child, so off we went. Then we got there, there was nobody there because it was early. Of course, we were paddling, running around, collecting crabs and everything, giving the young fella drinks of water out of the bottle and after a long time we decided to come home.*

What we didn't know was that everybody was out looking for us; they'd gone to the Customs House and couldn't find us. They thought maybe we'd fallen into the Liffey or something. Anyway, I came home, walking up the street with the child in the car and what I hadn't noticed was that the child was burned to a cinder with the Sun. We were burned as well and he was. I was walking down the road and all the shouting at me and the child's mother was going to hit me and my Auntie Mary run for her, "You're not hitting her". I was screaming "But we only went to Dollymount...." We'd been out the whole daylong and didn't realise it was coming to night time. You know in the summer; it was bright and you didn't know. Everybody was out looking for us. You know the way kids would be playing out and that and they don't realise the time. There was no such thing as having a watch then. The poor child must have been starving. Says my Auntie Mary to me, "Don't be minding that child, you're not taking him out anymore". And that was that, I never had to mind him again. I was only about ten years old at the time'.

My mother was always a very private woman who kept herself to herself. But there was nothing more that she loved than to have the gang of us sitting with her around the fire on a dark winter's afternoon, with the rain lashing on our kitchen window and the flames from the fire throwing up haunting shadows on to our ceiling. We would have arrived home from school, soaked to the skin from the rain and she would have our dinner on the table for us. Afterwards, we'd all sit on the floor around the fire at our mother's feet, hanging on to her every word as she told us of the Banshee that her own mother had seen when she lived in Tipperary and the ghosts that haunted the tenement houses and laneways of the old Monto area. And in particular, the ghost of the woman who was covered in a white sheet and who stood out in the corner of the backyard of the house where my mother's parents lived. She would have to go out into that yard every night, before going to bed, and fill a bucket with water from the outside tap for her father's tea in the morning. Her mother would hang out the window on the Landing to keep an eye on her just in case.

Originally, my mother was very hesitant in speaking to me while I had the tape recorder on, so I just left it on the kitchen table where we were sitting. After a few minutes I just knew she was bursting to tell me some story or other. She would usually begin with taking in a deep breath, raising herself up in her chair and say *"Did I ever tell you about..."* and off she'd go. So, I knew this day that I was on a winner because she just couldn't hold it in and eventually, to my great relief, told me to turn the recorder on. She spoke almost non-stop for the best part of two hours. Later, she was so delighted with the recording that she asked me to record herself and her sister together the following week. Unfortunately, and some time afterwards, my poor oul Ma' became too ill and never recovered, so that proposed recording never happened. However, I still have the original recording and sometimes, depending on my mood, I will lock myself away somewhere quiet and listen to my mother's voice, remembering the expressions on her face and the smile in her eyes, as she speaks to me out of the past. What a wonderful warm feeling it is, to experience still, after more than twenty years, the connection I had with the Ma' back then, through her storytelling.

Story Nine

The Flat

Some people will remember this building, situated on the corner of O'Connell Street and Abbey Street. It was the old *"Irish Permanent"*, but before that however and years ago, it was a Bank. My Da' worked here as a Porter in the early 1940's and told me of finding coins melted together from the fires in 1916. One day, the Bank Management people decided that it would be a good idea to have the Porter living on the premises as security. Now, at that time, himself and my Ma' had just moved into a front parlour room in a tenement house on Summerhill. The Ma' was delighted of course at having her own place and especially on the ground floor, no hauling babies and prams up the stairs.

The Bank Manager called my Da' into his office and told him the good news and said that he was to move himself and his family into the Flat on the top of the building, up in the attic, so to speak. My Da' wasn't too long out of the British Army and stood to attention as the Manager spoke to him and of course he knew he had to obey an order. But it didn't turn out to be that simple, the Bank Manager never reckoned how the Ma' would react at the thought of climbing up to the attic room several times a day with her brood. So, the Da' was chuffed with the idea and couldn't wait to let me Ma' know the good news and home he ran, all the way to Summerhill. He sat the Ma' down on the Tea Chest they used as a chair and told her about the move. The Ma' told me that he was probably expecting her to throw her arms around him in delight.

Instead, she said that she wasn't moving into any Bank, she had her own room and that was that. So now, the poor oul Da' was in a right pickle, stuck between two hard rocks. In the heel of the hunt, he moved into the Flat over the Bank, on his own and of course, that meant he had to feed himself as well. A couple of nights later he walked into his local Chipper for a *"One and One"* only to be met by his mother-in-law and her pals.

My Da' said it was like walking into a scene from *"The Gunfight at the OK Corral"*. By the time he left the Chip Shop he was well and truly hammered by the gang of Oul Ones for deserting his wife and young fambily (Family). The poor Da' sheepishly made his way to Summerhill with the fish and chips still slightly warm, a peace offering to the Ma'. She told me that she spied him out through the window, walking into the house and then she heard him knocking on the door of her room.

But being the Ma' she wasn't won over that easily with fish and chips. So, after a while and many words being spoken back and forward between the two of them, they settled down to eat the cold food on offer. The next day the Da' explained things to his Manager and that was the end of it, the Manager said that he understood and that it was probably for the best. My Da' said that he had to keep his head low for a good while after when dealing with the Manager or his mother-in-law.

Story Ten

Paddy and Bernard Coffey 1981

Striving to Survive

Although my father always worked, there was never an overabundance of money in our home. My mother was a very private woman and was never in favour of my father borrowing money from the Bank, which he would get, interest free, being a Bank employee, a Bank Porter. Instead my mother borrowed money from a legal money lender, a Jew man from Mary Street, now that's what he was known to us as back then. He would call to our home every Saturday morning for his payments and when we answered the door to him, he'd say, *"Tell your Mammy that the Jew man is here"*. In later years he went and fought in what became known as the *"Six Day War"* out in Israel.

My mother would always bring him into our front parlour so that he could do his business in private. It was only years later that I discovered my mother was acting as a kind of collecting agent for him and for which she never received any payment. There were many of our neighbours who also borrowed money from him but they didn't want him to be seen calling to their door, so my mother's front parlour took on the role of being a central point for each of the neighbours to bring their money and excuses to.

My father would also take on extra work to earn money. In the early years he worked Monday to Friday and half day Saturday in the Bank. The other half of Saturday was usually spent doing work for some of the bank employees, in their homes, painting and decorating or putting up shelves and the like. Most of these people lived in the Stillorgan area of north County Dublin and my father would cycle out to their houses from work and then home again in the late evening.

Most of my father's holiday time was spent working, putting up wallpaper for my mother or doing odd jobs for some of our neighbours, especially if there was a widowed woman who lived nearby and had no one to do the work for her. I remember when my mother started earning money by working at home. A large brown box would arrive at our house filled with plastic toiletry bags and a bundle of string. My mother would have us all sit around the kitchen fire attaching one piece of string to each bag. When she had them finished, a car would arrive out and collect them. There were of course other families that lived in our area who were worse off than we ever were and one family in particular would get our cast-offs or what was left of them.

I'm sure there were many times over the years when my parents were struggling financially and otherwise, much more than we were ever made aware of. I do recall times when my mother would refuse to sit down and eat with us, she'd make an excuse that she wasn't hungry from doing all of the cooking. I look back now and wonder was she making sure that she had enough food for my father's dinner when he'd arrive home from work.

Our Granny Burke, my mother's mother, lived with my Aunt Kathleen, my mother's younger sister, and Uncle Ned, not too far from where we lived. Ned worked in the ESB in Ringsend and Kathleen had a job in Bachelor's Food factory. Ned was always paid on Thursday. Because money was always scarce and there being little or no food in our house, on Thursday we'd often be sent to my Granny for our tea, we'd be given a cup of tea and two slices of bread and margarine. Sometimes Kathleen would send us home with a loan of money for my mother. Then on Friday, after my father would arrive home during his lunch time with his wages, my Granny would visit my mother and bring home the borrowed money to Kathleen. I suppose in this way my Granny was making sure that her two girls never had a falling out with each other over the money.

I have no memory of my father and mother ever having a row in front of us, they never used bad language in front of us either. Things may have changed in that respect after I left home at nineteen years of age. My father, on the odd occasion, would arrive home from work of a Friday evening with a few drinks in him but he was never violent or frightening. After his dinner he'd always fall asleep by the fire. My poor mother, similar to my father, never stopped going from one end of the day to the next. They were hard working people who took their parental responsibilities very serious.

To me, our neighbourhood was always an interesting place to be in, there were so many layers of social standing between those who had and those who hadn't. They all came under the heading of being "*Working Class*" and yet there were some of them that never worked and others that never wanted to. Some appeared to be very grand and even posh. In our eyes any families that had six children or less were always considered to be posh. We'd see some of our posh neighbours going off to Mass of a Sunday morning and they'd be all polished and shining like saints up in Heaven, the father with his Sunday hat on his head and his shoes all polished. And his wife linking arms with him like they were teenagers and her head scarf blowing in the early morning breeze as they heading off to nine o'clock Mass.

These were the type of people that always got to sit up at the front of the church and they used to stick out their tongues further than we ever could when the Priest would be giving out the Holy

Communion. And of course, they sang the loudest when the hymns were being sung, you could even hear them from down at the back of the church. And when the Holy Communion was finished being given out, they were always the loudest to cough, the whole church would be lifted up in a grand chorus of coughing in three-part harmony. All the men would be trying to outdo each other coughing and spluttering all over the place and sometimes if you were unfortunate enough to be sitting in front of a good cougher you might get it down the back of your neck. I remember trying to figure out who it was that started it all off, it must have been someone posh because the first cough always seemed to start up at the front and work its way towards the back. Maybe it was after the priest went back up onto the Altar and the Altar Boy rang his little bell.

President de Valera laid out in State 1975

Story Eleven

Fell Asleep

I remember my father telling me of one time when he fell asleep in church. You see, he always cycled to work and home every day, a distance of over six miles round trip in hail, rain and snow. He worked six and a half days a week back then. He did odd jobs for people he worked with.

On one Friday in particular he arrived home exhausted and after eating his dinner, was settling down in the only armchair we had at that time, for a well-earned snooze. It was then my mother reminded him that he had to go around to the Men's Sodality for eight o'clock. So off he went with one of the neighbours, Mister Hayes. They sat in near to the pulpit and the place was packed tight with all the men from our parish. Well, my father said he was sitting there, nice and cosy and half asleep, trying to pay at least some attention to the Priest rattling on about some sin or other, when he nodded off. Later on, his pal, Mister Hayes and himself had a good laugh about it.

Mister Hayes said that my father nodded off and resting his head on Mister Hayes's shoulder went totally into Noddy Land. Within seconds didn't my father let out a great big snort, from his snoring, all over the church and the Priest let out a roar that woke my father up with a jolt. *"If I find out who made that noise..."* roared the Priest into the microphone, *"...I'll send them to Hell"*. My father sat up with an innocent look on his face and looked around at the men behind him, pretending it wasn't him that snored. He said it was easily known that the oul Priest never did a hard day's work in his life.

Story Twelve

My father in Malta 1934

The Jarvey

Back in the late 1980's, and mainly in the winter months, on most Tuesday evenings, I would call over to spend time with my father while the Mammy went off to her Bingo. I'd always phone him first just to make sure he was up to a visit. This of course, gave him plenty of time to gather his thoughts together as to what stories he would want to tell me about his life growing up in Dublin since 1912, the year he was born. Many of the stories he would tell me I would have heard several times before but that didn't matter because there was always a chance that I had missed out on some small detail before. To me, every detail, no matter how big or small it was, was so important in the overall picture I was putting together of my father's life and that of his family. It's such a pity that I didn't have access to a tape recorder back then but I always brought a pen and paper with me for writing down notes and pieces of what he was telling me and later on I'd sit down at home and try to recreate his stories. Then the next time I'd check out the details with him.

He still loved the oul coal fire back then and he'd have it blazing for me when I'd arrive, having travelled over to him on two buses. He'd sit on one side of the fireplace with a glass of hot whiskey and I'd sit on the other with my mug of hot chocolate. This is kind of how it was in our family years ago when we didn't have a Telly, the Da' and Ma' would sit us all on the floor around the fire and tell us stories of how life was for them growing up in Dublin all them years back and how really poor their neighbours were.

They would talk about men on the run from the Black and Tans and doors in the tenement houses being smashed in by the rifles of soldiers and mothers and wives with their little children hanging out of their aprons, screaming and crying as they watched their husbands, fathers and sons being beaten black and blue. They would tell of the terror of coming face to face in the street with an army uniform, because most times or not, the children too were slapped in the face or given a kick for just being there. My Da' said there was terror around every corner back then.

Sitting together in our armchairs was like sitting in a *"Time Machine"* that brought myself and the Da' back to the scenes of his stories. I could almost smell the aroma of boiled cabbage, piss buckets, and rat droppings, all mixed with the blood, sweat and tears that flowed up and down the stairways of the tenement houses. Most of the stories I would have heard, from the Ma' and Da' over the years, mainly focused on their immediate family, neighbourhood and friends.

There was the time when my Da' was about ten years old and this Jarvey (An early form of Taxi Driver), came into Railway Street with his horse and cab, delivering his fare to one of the brothels in the area. My Da' said that this was one of the many ways himself and his pals had of earning a few bob. You see, the fare would go in one door and the Jarvey would go in another and while they were going about their business with the Girls, the Da' would keep an eye on the horse out on the street by holding his reins to stop him moving off too far. On this particular occasion a man came along and started roaring and shouting at the Da' for minding the horse, he said the Da' was encouraging people to go into the brothels. He then lashed out and gave my Da' a full force slap across the face.

Now, what this man didn't realise was, that there were two men standing nearby, who worked as Muscle Men for the Madam who ran the brothels where the Jarvey and his fare had gone into. My Da' said he was standing there roaring crying from the sting of the slap he had just got from this Oul Fella when the two lads approached your man and lifting him up off his feet, took him into the hallway of the tenement house where the brothel was and beat the living daylights out of him. They then emptied his pockets and gave his money to the Da' in way of compensation for the slap that he got in the face. Then they lifted the Da' up and put him sitting on the back of the horse out of harms way.

Soon enough, the Jarvey came out of the brothel, as did his fare, and they both fixing up their trousers, each of them gave the Da' a few pennies for looking after the oul horse. The Da' said he felt like a millionaire and ran home to his auntie, May Doyle and gave her all the money. His Auntie May and Uncle Sonny had reared him since he was about four years old. May handed him back twopence and sent him off to Mrs Meehan's shop to treat himself and his little cousins to a few sweets. The Da' said that your man that slapped him had probably been ripped off by another prostitute and he was still fuming when he saw my Da' holding the horse easy. Any time I'd ask the Da' how old he was when he started working, he'd always say he was ten years old and tell me this story.

Story Thirteen

The Scar

In recent times, one day I was sitting with my mother in her kitchenette when she said *"Do you want to see me scar"* Without waiting for an answer she rolls up the sleeve of her cardigan and shows me a tiny little scar on her arm. And of course, I had to ask what caused it. Then she got up and went into the parlour and returned with this photograph of herself on the right and her little sister, Kathleen on the left. She pointed at Kathleen and said *"It's all because of her"*. And then she settled down to tell me the story. Around the time that this photograph was taken my mother was no more than ten or eleven years old.

My mother and a gang of her pals were playing skipping out on the road and it was her chance to turn the rope. The girls were all lined up and ready to run in and take two skips each and then jump out on the other side. Her sister, Kathleen was playing *"Shop"* by the side of the road when another Young One came along and decided to do the same right next to her. Kathleen told her to move elsewhere because she was too near her. The young girl ran off crying because of what Kathleen had said to her. My mother was busy turning the rope and singing *"Looka whose coming down the street, Legser Murphy with Wah Wah feet..."* when, all of a sudden, she heard Kathleen roaring crying. My mother looked across the street to see a Young Fella about her own age and with no shoes on, kicking Kathleen's shop all over the road. He was the big brother of the little Young One Kathleen had told to move away.

My mother on the right with her sister Kathleen

Now, didn't my mother think that he had hit Kathleen. She said that she dropped the rope straight away and ran over to the Young Fella, grabbed him by the hair and gave him a few thumps. He ran off in through the doorway of one of the tenement houses.

As my mother and her pals were fixing up Kathleen's shop, she let out an unmerciful scream and grabbed her arm. She saw blood gushing out and looking up at the sound of laughter, saw the Young Fella she had boxed, looking out the window of the room where he lived and laughing at my mother in pain. He had flung down a piece of broken slate and hit her on the arm with it. She said that without even thinking about it she ran into the tenement house and up the stairs to the Young Fella and gave him another boxing.

Her pals took her to Temple Street Hospital where a Nurse cleaned her wound. She said that a Doctor came along and told her he'd have to give her a few stitches. As soon as his back was turned, she ran home and had her Auntie Mary put Iodine on it to stop the bleeding. Now, the Young Fella's mother came on the scene and threatened to box my mother. Her Auntie Mary, stepped in and put the run on your woman.

And there I was sitting in the kitchenette looking at my mother, who was as proud as Punch, showing off her scar. She would never let anyone hit or bully her little sister. After my father passed away, Kathleen would always visit my mother on the same day every week and they'd spend all their time talking about old times when they grew up in the Monto.

Story Fourteen

Coffin Material

This is my older sister, Vera Coffey, making her First Holy Communion in 1945. That table is in nearly every studio photograph I have of my family. I even have a photo of my mother standing at that very table when she was sixteen years old. Some people might already know the story behind Vera's First Holy

Communion outfit but for those who don't, I'll tell it again. With 1945 being the War Years or *"The Emergency"* as my father would call it, there was little or no money to go around and especially when it came to such a very special occasion such as a First Holy Communion. Now, I have to say, that my mother was never one for putting her hand out for help, so, when it came to dressing our Vera out for her First Holy Communion, my mother was in a quandary.

Our next-door neighbour, Granny O'Brien, used to work as a seamstress in Arnott's Fashion Shop but had to give it up when she married. She still had her own sewing machine, which she had bought when she originally started working there, that was the rule, each girl had to supply their own machine. Now, she also had a daughter who worked for a place over off Mountjoy Square that made Habits for laying out dead people in and they also made the lining for going inside the coffins.

One day, Granny O'Brien sent in for my mother and told her to bring our Vera with her. Well, in next to no time at all she had sewn up a most beautiful outfit for our Vera out of the material that her daughter had brought home from off the factory floor, the coffin lining. She even made a little handbag out of it as well. My mother made the veil out of some Net Curtain material that she had left over from when they first moved into our house all them years ago. Granny O'Brien made our Vera's stockings and knickers for her on the sewing machine as well.

Vera Coffey 1945

So, our Granny Burke, bought Vera's overcoat and shoes because Vera was her first grandchild and was named after the little girl our Granny lost, she was only three years old when she died.

We only ever knew the woman next door as *"Granny O'Brien"*, she wasn't really our granny but she was as good as. She was a widowed woman with grown up children, she was always dressed in black. My mother always made sure that one of us was around in case Granny O'Brien needed any shopping. Her daughter, Margaret or Aileen, as we knew her, was my Godmother. Granny O'Brien's husband used to work with his brothers in the Mountjoy Brewery, that was situated across the road from Croke Park. So, there you have it, our Vera and her First Holy Communion story.

An old Pound Note

Story Fifteen

Christina Coffey

Isle of Man in 1954

When I was small it wouldn't have been every day of the week that my parents got much time to spend on their own. However, in July of 1954 they went on a day trip to the Isle of Man and brought only one of us with them, my older sister, Chrissie, who was fifteen years old at that time. Most of the rest of us would have been farmed out to neighbours and relatives for the day. The older brothers were sent in to Sheriff Street to my father's sister and her family. Some of us younger ones were sent up the road to spend the day with our granny and anyone left was looked after by our eldest sister, Vera, and our neighbours of course would also throw an eye out in case any of us gave Vera trouble. And that's how it was back in those days, everyone helped out where they could.

My sister, Chrissie, remembered this trip so well because it was the first time ever that she had seen and tasted Doughnuts, a man was selling them by the side of the road in Douglas, the town on the Isle of Man where they landed from the boat. She said she was so excited at being picked out as the only one to go with the Ma' and Da' and it was even her first time on a real boat in the sea. And of course, like myself, my father made sure to bring his Box Camera with him to record the occasion. I love the shots that he took of this trip showing my sister in her Sunday best and my mother all happy and smiling because she was free of all us kids for the day.

At this stage of their marriage my parents had nine children, three girls and six boys. During all those years my mother never put on weight, she was always slim looking, they both made a very handsome couple, even if I say so myself. The day before this trip my sister and my mother were busy with needle and thread as they stitched and sewed their beautiful dresses for this auspicious occasion. They had cut out the pattern the night before and stayed up most of the night with the oul Singer Sewing Machine going ninety. My sister always made her own dresses and especially when she was old enough to go out dancing.

I can just imagine the freedom my parents must have felt as the boat pulled out from the quayside in Dublin, no screaming kids pulling at them, no neighbours coming in looking to borrow a cup of sugar or a match to light the fire, total freedom. I can clearly picture my father standing out on the deck looking out over the sea and remembering the time he sailed on a ship from the English port of Southampton to the island of Malta. It was 1932 and he was eighteen years of age and a soldier in the British Army. He was encouraged to join up, by Mister McNulty, one of the leaders in the Belvedere Newsboys' Club, which he was a member of. There was no work available in Dublin back then and it was suggested to my father that if he joined the army it would keep him out of trouble. This is probably what was going through his mind as they sailed across the Irish Sea.

And of course, with Chrissie running around the deck with some Young One or other that she had become instant pals with when boarding the boat, the Ma' and Da' must have almost felt like they were going away on honeymoon together. But of course, when they were married in 1938 there was no money floating around for a honeymoon.

The Ma' told me that, every Saturday as the Butcher was closing up shop, he'd knock on the door of their flat with some meat that he had left over from the week and give it to her, free of charge. She told me that little story when her and I were driving along Parnell

Street one day. Whenever I'd take her into town in recent years her mind would always take her back to her younger days and out would come all of her stories and the worse of it was, I was so busy driving and watching out for people stepping off the footpath, that I couldn't stop and write them all down. So, as soon as I got home, I'd have my pen and paper out and scribble down what I could remember of what she had told me.

I don't ever remember any other time that the Ma' and Da' got to go away together without any kids in tow. After this trip away the Ma' went on to have another six more babies. She almost became a permanent resident in the Rotunda Hospital where most of us were born. Now, I remember a little ornament that the Ma' kept in the China Cabinet, in our parlour, that they brought back as a souvenir of their day away on the boat together. It was a little thing made of chalk, like a round picture frame with a picture of a Tram from the Isle of Man in it. I wonder whatever became of that little piece, because like our parlour door, the China Cabinet was always kept locked.

That's where the Ma' and Da' had all their memories safely stored away under lock and key. I remember one time the Ma' allowed myself and some of my younger sisters into the parlour to have a good gawk at her display of memories and of course each little piece had its own special story to go with it. It is a pity I didn't have a tape-recorder back then to capture those stories. It was a wonderland of pure magic for us standing there hanging on to every word the Ma' said. As the years go by all of my Da's photos that he took over the years become more precious than ever before and each story to go with them becomes almost sacred.

So now, that's it for the time being. I'm off to warm up my *"Time Machine"* and see if I can go back to 1954 and board that ship to the Isle of Man to taste those Doughnuts my sister was so mad about.

My brother Bernard and the Ma'

Story Sixteen

The Honeymooners 1954

This is the day in 1954, when my parents went to the Isle of Man, for the first time. They were married in 1938, after he'd come out of the army. My mother was eighteen years old and my father was twenty-three when they got married. She worked in Mitchell's Rosary-Bead factory in Waterford Street and he' had a temporary job as a Bus Conductor in Clontarf Bus Garage. They moved in with my granny in Cumberland Street flats until they got a place of their own. My Da' had only recently left the British Army and was struggling, like most men of that time, to find permanent work. Then he got some Christmas work in the Postal Sorting Office.

My father never knew that he had an older brother named William and an older sister named Agnes, they were born and died as infants before he was born and it was only in later years that I found this out while searching through government records. His father remarried and his new wife gave birth to a little girl named Jane Catherine who was born very premature and died the following day. My father never knew about her either, now isn't that strange to think that?

My mother told me one time that people back then never spoke about the little babies and children that they had lost in infancy. She told me that babies who died years ago had to be brought by the father to Glasnevin Cemetery for burial on a Saturday morning. I checked this out with an old grave digger who started working in Glasnevin when he was fifteen. He told me that he remembers a queue of men lining up outside the gates of the graveyard of a Saturday morning, some of them on their way to work, waiting to hand in their little bundles wrapped up in a white sheet or a small home-made wooden box.

My mother also told me that my father made two little such boxes for a neighbour of ours who had lost little twins. She remembered putting her arm around the mother of these little infants and trying to console her at her loss as they watched my father and the baby's father carrying a little box each up to the graveyard in Glasnevin.

When I look at this photo of the pair of them in the Isle of Man they look as though they hadn't a care in the world. This is probably the first time as a married couple that they got to spend time together on their own. Do we ever know all the same what stories and experiences the older generation had to go through all those years ago?

My mother said that there was never a time in her life that she didn't know my father as they grew up in the same street together. At one time, when she was sixteen, she used to write letters for families that had sons in the British Army and she'd always write a little note of her own to them letting them know how their mother was doing and she did the same for my father's family. When a letter would arrive back from the son, all the neighbours were brought into the tenement room to hear my mother reading it out for the family, while they all sat around drinking tea and shedding tears because they missed him and were worried about him. My mother told me that she could read and write before she started off in school. My mother's Auntie Mary, had some experience as a trainee School Teacher in Terenure and she taught my mother to read and write.

And that's the way it was all those years ago when my parents took the boat over to the Isle of Man for a day trip, away from all of their worries and cares back home in Dublin in 1954.

Story Seventeen

The Wireless Set

Years ago, a radio was known as a *"Wireless"*. I remember one time when we had a wireless in our kitchen in Cabra West. Because our house was built during the war years the Corporation could only afford one socket per house. Later on, my father put in a double socket, now I'm not too sure how safe this was because he knew next to nothing about electricity, he just chanced his arm at it. So, everything electric was run from this one point and the main thing that was always plugged into it was our wireless. It wasn't a new wireless by any stretch of the imagination, it probably belonged to my Granda' Coffey and when he died, I'd say my father' got it and that's how we had it. According to him, the oul granda' and the stepmother used to love sitting by the wireless in the evenings listening to Radio Luxemburg, they lived in the front parlour of number 18 Lower Gardiner Street.

My mother loved the wireless as well and one of her favourite programmes was *"The Kennedy's of Castle Ross",* when this came on, we'd be all thrown outside to play so that the Ma' and my two older sisters could listen to it in peace. They would arrive home from work on their bicycles, the ones without the crossbar, during their lunch break. I remember before we got a telly the wireless would be on at night and we'd all be sitting by the fire listening to some story or other out of it. It was like being in the Picture House without a picture to look at, we just had to use our imagination. Now, one of the main problems with our old wireless, as it got on in years that is, was the main valve at the back became loose. So, while we'd be waiting ages for the thing to warm up and come on, one of us would usually put our hand in the back and tighten the valve, in the hope that it would come on quicker. This worked every time, except for that one time when the Da' got a shock from it.

You see, he was always the first up for work every morning, my mother was always the first one down the stairs because she would boil the kettle on the gas stove for his cup of tea and she would make him a piece of toast so that he had something in him for going out to work. On this one morning in particular however, he must have fallen back asleep for a few minutes because he jumped up out of bed roaring and shouting that he was late for work. Now, my mother already had his tea and toast ready for him, so he couldn't have been that much late, I think he just panicked at the idea of being late. He always hated the idea of being late for anything, he probably got that from his days in the army. And don't talk to me about if any of us were late if we had to meet up with him in town. Now, one of the things that was a part of my father's job as a Bank Porter was that he was always expected to be clean shaven, no matter what. But that was him all over, he wouldn't set foot outside of our house without being shaved and wearing his oul collar and tie, I think that might have been another army thing with him.

So, on this morning that he had himself convinced that he was late for work he decided it would be better if he had his shave downstairs in the kitchen sink rather than upstairs in the hand basin in our toilet (Modern day bathroom). There he was shaving away over the sink, his tea and toast on the table going cold and suddenly he remembers he never turned on the wireless to get the time. Now, this is where his whole day fell flat on its face before it had even started properly. He turned on the wireless and being as impatient as he was at that moment, he then put his wet hand into the back of the wireless to tighten the valve. It was at this very moment that he learned a very valuable lesson, never put a wet hand anywhere near anything electric.

My mother told me that there was an unmerciful bang out of the back of the wireless, followed by a big flash, when all of a sudden, all she could see was my poor father sailing across the kitchen, almost in slow motion and landing on the table, spilling his cup of tea and sending his piece of toast into the air. After a few minutes of complete silence, he eventually picked himself up off the table, put his coat on, grabbed his bicycle and headed out to work half shaven and still shaking from the experience. My mother told me that she had a little giggle to herself about it when he was gone off to work.

It was a few weeks later when my father arrived home one day with a brand-new wireless strapped onto the back of his bicycle. He got it on Hire Purchase from a place over in George's Street at two shillings and sixpence a month, he had a pal in the shop that arranged the repayments for him. So now, we no longer had a wireless, we had a *"Radio"* instead, that's what my father called it and it took pride of place in our kitchen. I remember him bringing some of our neighbours in to see it and listen to his new radio.

Our poor oul wireless was destined for my father's shed where he planned on fixing it someday. It was put with all the other things he was going to fix whenever he got a minute to himself, the hammer without a handle, the punctured bicycle tube, the Holy Mary Statue with the head broken off it, the oul kitchen chair that had only three legs, a pair of old shoes that needed new soles put on them, the box of bent nails to be straightened out, the rock hard paint brushes waiting to be cleaned and all those other bits and pieces that you could find back then in most sheds around Dublin. I don't know what eventually became of our old wireless set, it's probably up in *"Wireless Heaven"* somewhere, waiting for your man with the wet hands to come along.

Story Eighteen

Chrissie, Anne and Martin Coffey

Girl's Knickers

This could very possibly be my all-time favourite family photograph. It was taken sometime in the 1950's, probably 1955 and it says so much about our family situation in those years. At that time Ireland was still getting to grips with the ending of WWII and the rationing of food stuffs and fuel. Up to the early 1950's certain parts of *"The Emergency"* was still in place, such as having to use our Gas and Electricity sparingly. Up to 1951 the Gas Inspector was still going around to make sure families had their gas turned off after eight o'clock at night. This was a form of *"Lock Down"* with certain laws in place similar to what we've recently experienced here with the virus thing going around.

I used to love listening to my parents talking about *"The Emergency"* and thinking how strange it was that the world was at war but we weren't here in Ireland. And of course, a great big part of that era was the time in 1941 when the German's bombed the North Strand area of Dublin. Several other areas of Dublin had also been bombed but my father used to say that they were more or less out in the country, such as Terenure and the South Circular Road, that's probably because they were south of the Liffey, which was *"No Man's Land"* to the Da' back then. Do you see, my parents knew a lot of the families that had been bombed out of it and of course, like many other men and women back then, they went to see what they could do to help.

When this photograph was taken, they had a small family, there were only ten of us, six boys and four girls, there was another five more in the waiting lounge, so to speak. Now, my father was working and my mother was struggling to keep all our open mouths filled. Do you know, whenever I see a documentary about birds and the Mammy Bird surrounded by a whole load of little chicks with their mouths constantly open for a maggot or two, I always think of the poor Ma' and how she had to be like the Mammy Bird. At the end of the day my poor mother would be worn out and my father would nearly have to carry her up the stairs to bed.

In this photograph there are two of my older brothers out in the water, I think it's in Dollymount and there's my big sister Chrissie and my little sister Anne. Chrissie was working in a Sewing Factory at this time, she started there when she was thirteen years old and she was great at the sewing and the knitting. She always made her own dresses like the one in the picture and she would have knit the cardigan as well.

My mother always made sure that her girls were well able for the knitting, the crochet and the sewing. Chrissie told me that she never went out dancing in the same dress twice, she'd always sew up a new one on the day of the dance. She'd bring home a couple of strips of waste material off the factory floor where she worked and in next to no time at all she'd have a new dress. Her other dresses were usually given to the cousins down in Sheriff Street or else my mother would cut them up and make something for our Anne. That's how Anne has a fancy looking swim suit in this photo, it was made from one of Chrissie's throw off dresses.

And our Anne always had a great big yellow ribbon in her hair, no matter what the occasion, imagine going swimming with a ribbon in your hair? She was my father's little pet; she couldn't do any wrong in his eyes. I remember the time when my brother's pal, Eddie Mitchell had our Anne on the cross bar of his bike, one that he had made up himself from an oul frame that he'd found up in the dump. And there they were going great guns up and down our road and our Anne with a great big smile on her face and her yellow ribbon waving in the breeze, when *"a little snot"* of a young fella (Excuse the language) ran out and jammed a stick in between the spokes on the front wheel. That's when all hell broke loose as our Anne went flying up and over the handle bars and landed on her head, with a great big thump, in the middle of our road and poor Eddie went skidding off the bike and cut the knees off himself. Our Anne had to go to hospital in an ambulance and her lovely yellow ribbon covered in blood.

The other thing about this photograph of course, is myself on the right, wearing a pair of girl's knickers. Now, they could have belonged to either one of my older sisters or maybe one of my cousins from Sheriff Street but there's no doubt about the fact that they were miles too big on me. Sure, can't you even see the nappy pin holding them up where my mother had twisted them around my little skinny waist? It never made any difference to me back then what I was wearing on one of our day trips out to Dollymount and the beach. I just remember the freedom we had of running wild up and down the beach and splashing each other in the water and the taste of salt and sand in the sambo's my mother had brought to feed us with. We would have eaten anything back then, cooked or uncooked, with the hunger on us from the fresh open air and the sea breeze in our little faces.

We used to love running across the old wooden bridge and seeing the sea water down below and we all in fear of our lives in case we slipped in between the great big wooden beams that formed the bridge. The older brothers were like Geronimo and his warriors galloping off to see who would be first to get to the sandy beach.

I can still see my mother pushing the pram with my baby sister Mary inside, you could barely see her with all the stuff that was piled up on the pram. And my father, of course, with a fag in the corner of his mouth, cock of the walk so to speak. Him and the Ma' talking about old times and how they too were brought to Dollymount by their parents and my father was a great swimmer, he even had medals for life saving that he got when he was in the British Army in Malta. All of the troubles of daily living and struggling for my parents were left under the stairs on the number 30 bus on the days that we went to Dollymount.

Dollymount Strand

Story Nineteen

When I was Sick

I never liked being sick when I was a little boy, because I had to stay indoors and I couldn't go out to play with my pals. Sure, even now I hate being stuck indoors. All my brothers and sisters would have gone off to school and I was left in bed on my own. There was never a noise outside because my pals as well were all in school. My mother would come up the stairs to check on me and make sure I was comfortable before she headed off to the shops to get her messages. It was only on the rare occasion that a doctor was involved in any of us being sick, my mother would consult with my Granny or our older next-door neighbour, as to what she should do.

And if it was a Friday my father would arrive home from work with a great big bottle of Lucozade for whoever was sick. That was always sure to get us back up on our feet fairly quick and sometimes he'd even bring us home a Comic to read while we were in bed. I used to keep my comic under my pillow. I used to love reading about Dennis the Menace and his dog Gnasher or about Desperate Dan and his Cow Pie with a pair of cow's horns sticking out of it. The comic was always guaranteed to cheer me up no end.

Two of my brothers used to always sleep beside me at night when we had to go to bed but when I was sick, they had to sleep at the foot of our bed, down the far end. My brother Noel used to always tell us ghost stories before we'd go to sleep, he used to make them up as he went along but we didn't know that until years later. I remember him telling us a haunty story about a hand that would come in through the window and crawl into our bed and we'd be roaring in terror until my father would come up and tell us to get to sleep. And even then, Noel would be running his hand up and down our legs to frighten us. But if one of us little ones became ill it would do the rounds of the rest of the family. I remember when my sister Anne got the measles and my father says *"I hope it's not German Measles"*. That was the worst thing you could get according to the Da' because his cousin fought against the German Army during WWII. Sure, us kids didn't know the difference, measles was measles and meant confinement in bed for a few days, a terrible experience altogether.

I remember one time when I was nearly better and my mother let me little pal, Willier Kavanagh, come up the stairs to see me. I was delighted of course to see him and he started off telling me about a scrap between two boys in our school yard and how the headmaster broke up the fight with his cane. I was raging at missing all the excitement. Willier was my bestest ever pal in school and we started off in the convent when we were only four years old and we were holding hands as we walked up our road because we thought we were big boys now. Willier is with Holy God now and I still think of him and all the great times we had as kids playing cowboys on the railway and kicking an oul tin can for a football.

Sure, I remember the many times him and I would sit at our kitchen table after school and my mother would feed us both. But once I became better from being sick, I was like a wild stallion trying to break out of his corral in a cowboy film, I'd be after bursting a gut to get outside and play. My mother would be standing at our hall door watching me climbing over our front gate with a look on her face that said *"Who's next"?*

Story Twenty

Easter Eggs

I will always remember Easter Sunday morning in our house when I was growing up. It was almost like a second Christmas Day for us because my father would serve each of us a boiled egg with a face drawn on it and our name spelled across it. He would have at least twelve to fourteen eggs boiling in the one pot and all with a different face and name. This was the only time of the year that we got a boiled egg. After breakfast we were all shipped off to ten o'clock Mass. It always seemed to go on forever because we'd be dying to get home for our chocolate Easter Egg.

In my Da's job as Bank Porter he came to know each and every shopkeeper and business owner in the Camden Street area. This always proved very useful and especially at Christmas time or Easter because he would always get the Easter Eggs at a bargain price.

My Da' was a *"Back Scratcher"* where useful people were concerned, he would do little favours for them throughout the year and they, in return for him, whenever he needed one done. Sometimes he would also arrive home with a large box of chocolate marshmallow eggs and we'd get maybe two or three each. This was great, because we could tell all our friends that we got four Easter Eggs each and they'd be mad jealous.

And still to this day, every Easter Sunday without fail, I draw a little face on my egg and put my name on it, in memory of my Da'.

Happy Easter

Story Twenty-One

My Dad's Football Team 1946

Do you remember?

I remember a time when my older brothers and a gang of lads went door to door collecting old newspapers, empty bottles and jam jars, that they'd bring for recycling to a man down off North King Street, we used to call him Harry Littleman but I don't think that was his real name. And the lads always made sure to drain out any bottles with a drop of whiskey or gin still in the bottom of them. I well remember the oul scrap dealer used to place his foot under the weighing scales and move it in such a way as to show the weight of the waste paper in his favour. The money the boys they got from him was quickly spent on sweets.

Myself and my pal used to bring empty lemonade and stout bottles back to the pubs or the shops and we'd get a few pennies for them. There was a scrap man in Smithfield who used to give us a pigeon instead of money and when we'd get home and let the pigeon out, it would always forget to come back to us, my father used to call them *"Homing Pigeons"* because they always went home where they came from.

We walked everywhere as kids without fear of man or beast, we'd walk into town to have a look around Woolworths or Hector Greys shops or go up to the Phoenix Park collecting chestnuts or conkers as we called them back then. Some of my older brothers and their friends used to swim in the canal with dead dogs floating on top of the water or a sack of drowned kittens bobbing up and down and there was always lots of old bicycle frames and baby prams with no wheels on them, in the water, as well as rats the size of a large cat.

We'd often let a dog lick the sores on our knees to make them better. And if you had a loose tooth my father or one of the older brothers might tie a piece of thread around it and tie the other end onto the door handle and then you had to wait for someone to open the door from the other side and *"WHAM"* the tooth would be pulled out, (No Root Canal work needed then?).

We often ate orange skins that we picked up off the ground and apple butts too, my brother smoked cigarette butts that some Oul Fella had thrown away and sometimes you'd be sucking on a sweet and then let your pal have a suck on it too, the same with your chewing gum. During the interval in the Picture House, after watching some cowboy who fell off his horse and was dragging himself to the river for a drink of water, we'd go down under the seats looking for an empty ice cream tub and take it to the toilets with us to get a drink of water, we'd flush the big toilet and catch the water in the tub as it came down from the overhead cistern.

When my mother was cutting up a head of cabbage of a Sunday, she'd dig out the heart and cut it up between a few of us to eat raw. And if she boiled the scrap of ham in the cabbage water, we'd get a cup of that salty water to drink because it was full of iron. Sometimes we'd go into the farmer's field and rob the turnips and eat them raw. In the winter time we'd get pig's cheek for our dinner or maybe my father would arrive home with half a pig's head and that would be boiled up of a Saturday night.

And sometimes my father and mother would sit by the fire listening to the radio of a Sunday night eating pig's feet or Crubeens as my father used to call them. My most favourite things of all to eat was the Cow's Tongue and Cow's Heart or Ox Tongue was also delicious, we only got that on special occasions. Most Fridays during summer we got a bowl of rice for our dinner, that had been boiled in milk and we'd get a great big dollop of jam to mix in with it. Also, in the summer we always got salad sandwiches for our dinner on a Saturday, two slices of bread with a leaf of lettuce and some chopped up onion and Salad Cream in between them. My mother's sister got the Salad Cream for us out of Bachelor's factory where she worked.

In the winter months we got a bowl of porridge before we went to school each morning, the porridge was steeped in water overnight and then boiled up in the morning. Sometimes the porridge came in big lumps, depending on my mother's mood. Some Fridays, depending on the household cash flow, my mother would send a few of us to the local Chipper for six or eight bags of chips with loads of salt and vinegar. When we got them home, she would cut each bag in half with the bread knife and give us one half each for our dinner. We would always lick the vinegar and salt off the chip bag.

On Easter morning we all got a boiled egg each with a face drawn on it by my father and with our names on it as well. On Christmas morning we got a fried egg and a rasher with a slice of fried bread. Everything was washed down with tea, either in a jam-jar, as in the early days that is, or in later years, a cup that either had a crack in it or a chip missing out of it. Some of our cups we got from the Rag Man who used to come around our road on his ass and cart collecting rags, bottles and jam jars. I gave one of them my First Holy Communion suit for a balloon on a stick with a coloured feather on it, my mother never let me forget that one.

My mother used to make short trousers for us boys out of old overcoats my father or herself was finished with, if they didn't go on the bed first to keep us warm that is. My auntie Kathleen gave my older sister a jumper she had worn for a number of years and when the sister finished with it my older brother started wearing it.

Boys only wore Longers, long trousers, when they went out to work; my two eldest brothers wore trousers that belonged to my father. When the brothers went swimming, they either went in their nude or wore a pair of our older sister's knickers.

For a while, my older sister and her new husband came to live with us, they slept on the bed-settee in our parlour. When they came home from their honeymoon they moved in with his family. His mother told my sister that she'd have to sleep on their sofa and himself could sleep in with his brothers upstairs. When my sister told that to my mother, there was an order placed straightaway for a bed settee on hire purchased from Cavendish's at seven shillings and sixpence a week, my sister and her husband were moving in with us.

I remember on the first Saturday that they moved into our parlour, all of us kids were curious of course because we had never seen my sister in bed with a fella and so we all piled into the room where she and her new husband were sleeping. The other strange thing was that he had a head of blazing red hair, we never had anyone living in our house with red hair before. So, there we all were standing around the bed-settee when my mother appeared at the parlour door. Before she had time to open her mouth we were gone, scattered around the house, in fear of getting a wallop.

We didn't have a fridge back then either. The milk was kept in the back porch to stop it going sour. My mother shopped every day for bread and things for our dinner. Most families in Dublin had to do that because almost everything was delivered to the shops on a daily basis. Nothing in our kitchen ever went to waste. Anything we didn't eat our dog did.

At Christmas time my mother made her own puddings and hung them up in pillowcases out in the back porch. She'd always make one for our next-door neighbour. We would all get a go at stirring the pudding and making a wish and a lick of the wooden spoon. She also made her own Christmas cake. My poor mother was always on the go. If my father had trouble with his stomach ulcers, or Ulsters as we used to pronounce it, my mother would boil up some tripe, that's the lining of a cow's or sheep's stomach, in milk and pepper, for him. When one of the older brothers had a great big bile on his back my father got a bottle with hot water in it and placed it over the bile, as the water cooled down it caused a type of suction and sucked out all the poison in the bile. I think this was one of his old army cures. And we used to put mustard on a chilblain on our heels that we'd get from being out in the snow. And that's the way it was all those years ago.

Best of Pals

Story Twenty-Two

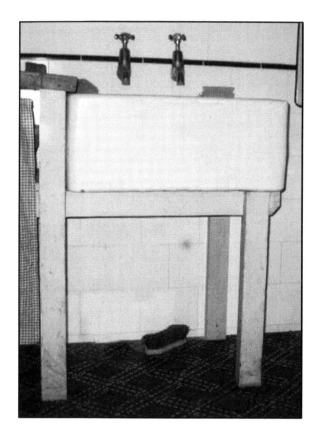

A Christmas Memory

Now, it may seem strange to some people for me to remember this but it's almost like it happened yesterday. I remember standing in our Belfast kitchen sink when I was about five years of age and the older sister giving me a good scrub in preparation for Santy on the night before Christmas. Then she got me to stand up and step out onto the kitchen chair, the only one we had at that time, and she drying me in the half of an old bed sheet. She asked me what Santy was going to bring me and I told her I wanted a cowboy suit with a gun and holster. She then put me standing by the fire to get a heat before going up to bed. And now she started washing my little sister, Anne.

When I was all dried, my big sister put my vest on me because that's all I wore back then to bed, she took me in her arms and carried me up the stairs. She told me that I'd have to kneel down beside the bed to say my prayers and ask Holy God to tell Santy what I wanted.

Over the years my father used to write all the letters to Santy for us little ones who couldn't write, it was gas when I think of it because there was no such thing as a Biro or that, he had to use a pen and ink and he'd put some ink on one of our fingers and get us to press it on our individual letters so that Santy would know which of us it was from. I think this was something he had learned in the army.

I remember so well standing by the blazing fire that my mother had put together with an old shoe and a bucket of slack and cinders and bits of potato skins and stuff like that and gazing up in wonderment at our Christmas Tree. It was pure magic for a five-year-old to see the fairy lights glowing in the semi darkness of our kitchen.

I suppose in some way it was what I imagined Heaven would be like. My mother would take down her home-made pudding that was handing up in our back porch in a pillow case and cut a slice for Santy while my father poured out a glass of Stout for himself and of course poor oul Rudolph with the red nose had to be included, he got half a carrot, the older brother ate the other half.

I know now that back in the 1950's my father and mother certainly didn't have much and I'm sure we barely got by on what they did have but they never let us down when it came to Christmas. The poor mother would sit up half of the night looking after the bit of meat and the skinniest turkey you ever saw, that was cooking in our gas oven. My father would be there playing his part in helping to clean and tidy the place because Baby Jesus was about to arrive at any minute. And sure, our few decorations were always the same ones that went up every year. We had a little cardboard Santy that opened out and his fat belly would stick out and we had an Angel with a smiley face as well.

And do you know, the poor Ma' and Da' would only be gone to bed when the older sisters and the brothers would shake us little ones out of our sleep and carry us quietly down the stairs to see what Santy had brought for us. And there would be all the presents beautifully wrapped and laid out with our individual names written on pieces of paper and placed on the presents.

And do you know what, Santy used to write the exact same way as my father, isn't that strange or what? Well now, wait till I tell you something, when I opened my present there it was, a little Cowboy Suit with a hat and a shiny silver gun in a plastic holster, I was so excited that I started crying. Then I put my hand into my stocking that was on the floor beside the fire and I took out a whole orange, I was laughing and crying all at the same time. Now, that's what Christmas is all about.

Story Twenty-Three

Dear Santy

I have tried me very best to be good for me mudder all year and I even went to Confession last Saturday. I only had a few sins to tell the priest so I made some up. My teacher in school told me that I'm the best eejit he ever had in his class and told me I'd go far, probably as far as England. I helped me Da' to clean up his shed last week by putting all his rusty screws in a jam-jar to keep them tidy. Sometimes I try to help my little sister with her homework so the Nun won't give her a slap. Me mammy told me to write my letter to you and to stick it up the chimbly before she lights the fire. When our baby cries, I try to be the first to put the soother in his mouth. He nearly always cries when my older brother puts the dog in the pram beside him. He gets full of flea bites and me Ma' has to put vasaleen on them. My pal got the measles and we spent hours counting all the little red things on his belly. My other pal from across the road went mitching from school last week.

For christmas this year I would like a train like the one in the picture and a cowboy suit as well, if that's not too much to ask for. And please put an orange in me stockin' because I like them very much. I'll ask me mammy to leave you out a drink and a piece of her pudding and a carrot for Rudolph the red nose raindear. And I'll do me best to be good for the next time as well.

Thank you and good night Santy

Martin x

Story Twenty-Four

A Canal Walk with the Da'

It was always around this time of year, October to November, on a winter's day, that my father would take us for a good stroll up along the Royal Canal. Up over Broombridge we'd go and turning right, we'd make our way towards Liffey Junction and head on to Cross Guns Bridge in Phibsborough. Whatever hats and coats we could find, it didn't matter if they fit us or not, we'd put them on. And the younger sisters with their scarves, that they had knit in school, around their necks and their hats that my mother had shown them how to crochet on their heads. And off we'd go up the road and away on an adventure with our father.

I can still see him with his hands shoved into his pockets, his head held up high with his cap tilted to one side and a cigarette sitting in the corner of his mouth. Us younger ones would run ahead of him, not too far mind, as the Ma' had told him to be sure to keep an eye on us going up by the waters of the canal.

How easily pleased we were then and how exciting it was to have our father take us out for a good long walk. I think he needed a break from all the painting and decorating he was doing in our house in preparation for Christmas. And as sure as anything as soon as we'd eventually get home the Ma' would have the Christmas Pudding mix ready and waiting for each of us to take our turn at stirring it and making a wish. I always wished that Santy would bring me what I had asked for in my letter that was already up the chimbly.

As we walked along the canal my father would be telling us stories of when he was a young fella and how it was in this very canal that he first learned to swim in his nude with all his little pals. We'd all break up laughing at the idea of our father in his nude. And he'd tell us that he was only four years old when his Mammy died and how sad he was then because he wasn't allowed to go to the graveyard to see her being buried. I remember when we saw all these swans on the canal and my father telling us about the Children of Lir and how their stepmother turned them into swans. He had a stepmother too he told us but he didn't like her because she wanted to put him and his brothers into Artane and to give his sisters to the Nuns.

These are some of the things my father would tell us about and then he'd start singing some of the songs he'd learned when he was in the British Army all those years ago and we could sing some of them as well because he sang them every Sunday morning when he'd be shaving in the toilet upstairs, it's called a bathroom now. After he died our neighbour told me that she missed my father singing of a Sunday morning, she said she could hear him through the toilet wall, singing at the top of his voice.

Now, most times when we'd get home from our walk, we'd be freezing but we didn't feel the cold and we knew that our mother would have a great big blazing fire on the go and at least two home-made apple tarts on the table for us to have at tea time. So, as soon as we'd be finished stirring the Christmas Pudding it was put into a pillow case and hung up in the old porch, then we'd all give a hand to set the table for our tea.

And do you know, after we had cleaned up from our tea we'd gather around the fire and most of us would doze off asleep. My mother would sit on one side of us and her knitting needles would be click clacking away while my father was snoring in the armchair, there wouldn't be a sound out of all us little chickens sitting around the fire. Now, this Christmas I'm asking Santy to bring me a *"Time Machine"*, like the one I saw in the Picture House years ago, because I want to go back and take loads of photographs of how we were as a family back then and maybe include some of me little pals and the stuff they got from Santy and a photograph of my father snoring in his armchair as well. That's my wish for Christmas.

Story Twenty-Five

My little sister Mary on the right

Why Can't I remember?

It is interesting, that of all the stories and events I can remember from my childhood growing up, the one I have no memory of and which was probably the most traumatic in my early childhood years, are the events surrounding the time I was knocked down and almost killed. There is perhaps one little snippet of memory that I have, which took place after the event, that I remember. It probably only lasted about two or three minutes or maybe even less. In my mind I can clearly see myself sitting on a chair in our old kitchen and my left leg is in plaster. I am sitting right next to the door that leads out into our hallway. I can see my older brother, Billy, lifting me and the chair over to the kitchen table and then nothing. I have no memory of the actual accident or being in hospital, I was four years of age at that time.

There was a series of events that happened on that particular day, the date of which I have no idea. It must have been on Friday lunchtime when the first incident happened. At that time my father worked as a Bank Porter in the Bank of Ireland on College Green. Why I say it must have been on Friday is because I remember that was the one day in the week when my father would arrive home on his motorbike from work, during his lunch break, and hand his weeks wages to my mother, he did this every week back then. My mother was then in a position to buy food to feed us all, the whole nine of us and the new baby.

The story I was later told over many years by my parents and some of my older siblings, is as follows. My father drove his motorbike across the Liffey and into Queens Street. As he was speeding up this street a car drove out from the junction with Haymarket, this leads into Smithfield, the car drove directly across the path of the oncoming motorbike. The bike crashed into the side of the car and the force of the impact sent my father hurtling through the air and in through the window of McGettigan's pub on the corner of the junction. My father told me that the Barman and some of his customers lifted him up off the floor and the barman handed him a glass of whiskey. Because of this drink the Garda later tried to charge him with drunk driving but the Barman went along and explained the situation to them.

Word eventually reached my mother telling her of the accident and of my father being taken to the Mater Hospital. Straightaway she went next door and told her neighbour the news. She then organised for my older sisters to take over looking after the baby and the rest of us, however, my ten-year-old brother, Noel, was told to look after me. Now, Noel and his little gang of pals had already made plans to do something and that something certainly didn't involve me tagging along, they had planned to go off and rob an orchard somewhere up off the nearby Navan Road. Now, it wasn't unusual back then for Noel and his pals to take me with them on some of their adventures, particularly if they involved a trip to the Phoenix Park.

While the older boys were busy discussing their moves and tactics for skinning an orchard of its apples, I was happily following behind, lost in a little world of my own. At some point in time and according to Noel's account, the lads ran out and across the main road. I was some way behind them and stepping out onto the road, without having the sense to look left or right, I stepped into the path of an oncoming small van belonging to the South of Ireland Asphalt Company. Noel said he heard the screech of brakes and looking behind him, saw me hurtling through the air and landing head first onto the road several feet away from the van.

Nelson's Pillar 1966

An ambulance was sent for and I was taken to Temple Street Children's Hospital. I have no memory of any of this. Noel and his pals had to forgo their plans to rob the orchard and hurry home to tell my mother what had happened. She wasn't at home of course but when she did arrive home the neighbour told her not to take her coat off. Now, while my mother was on her way to see me in hospital another of my older brothers fell and broke his arm. He ended up in the same hospital as my father. It's a wonder my poor mother didn't end up in the asylum in Grangegorman.

My mother told me that when I was unconscious, she was informed by the medical team that there was every chance that I wouldn't recover from the accident. I had a fractured skull, a broken leg, a broken collar bone, broken ribs and cuts and scratches everywhere. My mother also told me that she was never happy with how my leg was after the doctor's had later removed the plaster. She told me that it just didn't seem right to her. She mentioned this to the doctor but he just dismissed her concerns, until one day that is. My mother said that she was determined to have my leg x rayed and reset to her satisfaction. She told the doctor that she was not leaving the hospital until someone looked at my leg. They did and she was right. So, I had to get another plaster of Paris on my leg after it was reset. And still I don't remember any of this. What I do remember however, is my mother taking me to the hospital once a month every month for quite some time afterwards to have my leg checked out. I also remember that she bought me a comic each time we went to the hospital.

I still find it strange that after all these years I have no memory of anything relating to the actual accident and my stay in hospital. Maybe when my head hit the ground a delete button in my brain was set off. For many years my father kept a little pocket diary of certain family events, birth dates, how much we each weighed at birth, the number on my older sister's bicycles in case they were ever stolen, wedding dates and of course the little note he had written so many years ago to remind me that when I was twenty one I had to go and see a particular solicitor because my Dad had put in a claim for me for the accident. I was to get one hundred and fifty pounds. Now, back at the time, all those years ago, when the accident happened, that was a small fortune but by the time I was twenty-one it only amounted to about two hundred and fifty pounds.

Every time my father had cause to take out his little diary, he'd call me over to have a look at the entry with my name on it and out the story would come again. And then he'd tell me about the corset he had to wear from his accident, he had serious injuries to his back and had to wear it for a number of years. His face would always scrunch up and this painful look would come across it as he put a hand behind his back and placed it on where he had felt the most pain. It almost seemed as if he had gone back in time to the day of his crash. I'd ask him if he was still in pain and he'd smile and tell me that it's long healed now, and then he'd be better, just a funny little moment between the two of us. Sometimes he'd pull up his trouser leg to show me a scar on his knee that he got when he was a young fella when his pals got into a scrap with a gang of lads from

Foley Street. Or the one he had on his hip from when he tripped while climbing up a pyramid in Egypt when he was in the British Army. And once the army was mentioned he'd start off telling me all about the tattoos he had on his arms and where he got them from. His little pocket diary was always a great source of storytelling. I wish I had it today to see if I missed any story or other. So, that's my memory loss incident from all those years ago when I was only four years of age.

The top floor, on the right, where my parents lived in 1945

Story Twenty-Six

Tea Time 1950's

Dinner time or tea time arrangements in our house in the 1950's was always very much the same, my father and mother sat up at the head of the table, the two youngest children were at the end, there were four of us older ones on each side, and a baby over by the fireplace, a total of eleven children in all. Each of us had a place allocated to us at the table, the golden rule was never to take anyone else's place or there'd be war. *"Ma', he's standing in my place".*

"No, I'm not, there's plenty of room anyway". And all it took to sort things out was that special look the Ma' had, when you got that eye you knew you were next to getting a clout. The Da' had his tone of voice, it would go very low and his eyebrows would go into a frown and that's when we knew to back off. Now, the way it worked at the table was, the older two sat next to the Ma' and Da' and in order of age we all took our places, I was always near the end. Two of my younger sisters sat at the end of the table and when I say sat, I mean that the rest of us had to stand because we didn't have enough chairs for us all to sit down. Over time a couple of tea chests were introduced along with a small wooden bench the Da' made but for most of the time we had to stand. The youngest sister, the baby, was in the Moses Basket beside the fireplace and near to the Ma'.

Over time of course the dynamics would change around the table in accordance to whoever took the boat and emigrated to England, which was always the older ones. When this would happen there was always a shift up along the table as their place was taken by the next in line. We didn't have a teapot as such, we had a tea kettle, a great big one and only the older ones were allowed to lift that to pour out our tea. The Ma' always got the only cup that didn't have a crack in it and the Da' had his oul army mug, as he called it. In later years I had my own cup that I got out of the Pillar Café in O'Connell Street, it was a white Pyrex coffee cup, that was mine and no-one else was allowed to use it. Most of the cutlery we had, came from various hotels, restaurants and cafes from around Dublin and Bray.

The Da' always used the knife and fork that came out of the Gresham Hotel. One of the brothers had a knife, fork and a soup spoon that came from a hotel in Bray where he used to take his Moth dancing. The Ma' would always stir her tea with a small Apostle spoon from a set she was given as a wedding present all those years ago, she wasn't too fond of sugar in her tea. Whenever nobody was looking one of us or other would shovel a spoon of sugar into our mouth and run outside in case we were caught.

I don't ever remember us having butter on our bread back then, I think it was always margarine, *"the poor man's butter"* the Da' would call it. Most evenings for our tea we got a cup of tea and a few slices of bread and margarine, there was never any second helpings. During the week us younger ones got our dinner when we came in from school. That was always gulped down in seconds because we'd be bursting a gut to go out and play with our pals. The Da' and the older ones that were out working got their dinner when they came home, usually at about six o'clock. Saturday in our house was very laid back. If we came in hungry, we'd usually grab a slice of bread and a drink of water out of the tap at the kitchen sink and we'd be gone out again in next to no time. Dinner was usually mashed potatoes and beans with a sausage stuck in the potatoes.

We only ever stayed indoors whenever it was raining and even then, it had to be lashing down out of the heavens. The poor oul Ma' was constantly standing over the gas stove cooking and baking to feed a never-ending row of little and big mouths standing around our kitchen table. My two older sisters were very often roped in to help her. After our dinner or tea, we all had to do our bit in the washing up of the delph and cleaning of the table and the sweeping of the floor. The Ma' would be exhausted at the end of the day, she was on the go around our house twenty-four seven. The Da' was always out working, he never had just the one job, he had two or three and sometimes a fourth one as well.

Most Sundays after dinner we'd be sent to the Picture House and I suppose that was when the Ma' and Da' were able to get a breather before we'd come home again. Some Sundays but not every Sunday, the Ma' would make a couple of apple tarts for our tea and because there were so many of us, we'd only get one slice each. As we grew up and went out to work there was of course more money coming into the house and I'm sure that relieved some of the worry and pressure on the Ma' and Da'.

The Da' would spend most Sunday nights writing letters to the older ones that had emigrated to England. Some nights, as arranged with the older sister in England, he'd go to the nearest telephone box and give her a call in the hospital where she was working. She'd bring him up to date on the rest of them living over there and he'd report back to the Ma' while the rest of us sat around the fire listening to what he had to say.

Once nine o'clock came we were given our marching orders and told to go up to bed. By ten o'clock the Ma' and Da' could be heard dragging themselves up the stairs step by step, exhausted and worn out. We were a bit like the Walton's off the telly, because anyone that was still awake when the Ma' and Da' eventually reached the top of the stairs would hear *"Goodnight Mammy, goodnight Daddy"* from one of the sisters or one or two of the brothers would shout out *"Good Ma'. Da' don't forget to give me a call for work in the morning"*. *"Goodnight..."* the Ma' would answer *"...go to sleep now"*.

And that's what made the world go around for us in our house, the daily comings and goings that were not much different to most of our neighbours. The Ma' and Da' were like two oul plough horses equally yoked, pulling and sharing the same load week in and week out. God bless them, they were great people.

Old School Ink-Wells

Story Twenty-Seven

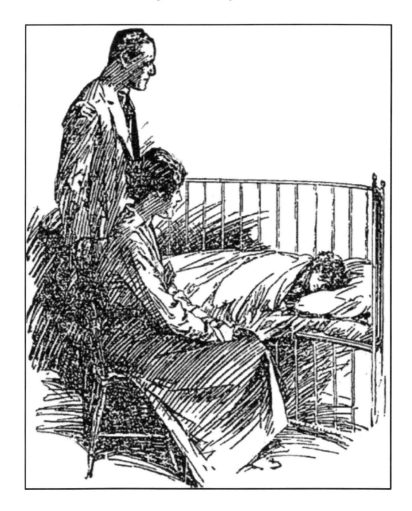

The Virus

It's a strange world we're living in at the moment all the same. I can't go out here or I can't go out there. Don't be talking to this one or don't be talking to that one. I'm standing too near or I'm standing too far. It almost reminds me of when I was a little boy all them years ago and I had the Flu. I couldn't go out then either and all my little pals shouting up to the bedroom window and asking me was I going for a ramble with them up to the canal to catch Pinkeens. Sometimes I would sit up by the window and look out at them all playing away and there'd be my sisters and all their pals playing skipping and piggy beds and shop and mammies. My gang would be out there playing Cowboys and Indians and running up and down our road with their bicycle hoops having a race and some of them would be standing at our gate having a whistling competition to keep me entertained. One of them would get up on our railings and do a balancing act or try to walk along the railings without falling off. There they'd be having great gas altogether and me stuck up there in bed with the Flu. It just wasn't fair.

I remember the time when my best pal, Willier Kavanagh, knocked on our hall door and gave my mother a bunch of comics for me to read, he'd found them up in the Dump near the canal. Some of them were a little bit damp and others had some muck on them but my mother didn't seem to mind, she told me to watch the bed sheets and not to get them dirty. I sat up in the bed and became lost in all the adventures in between the pages of the war comics and especially fighting the Arabs with Monty and his lads in the desert during WWII. There was one story I was reading about a submarine and I ducked under the covers with my torch on so I could feel what it was like in that cramped space below the sea.

I loved Winker Watson and his school blazer, we never wore blazers to my school and I used to have a great laugh at Desperate

Dan when his mother would serve him up his dinner of cow pie and the cow's horns would be sticking out of it. I suppose the one I really loved the most was The Bash Street Kids because they always reminded me of the little gang I was a member of. Sure, we'd always be in trouble for getting up to devilment on the Parish Priest or the Nuns or making fun of the shopkeeper who sold Nancy Balls. One time we set fire to a neighbour's hedge in his front garden because he wouldn't give us back our ball that had been kicked over the side wall of his house. I don't know what it was about robbing orchards but we always seemed to end up with sour cooking apples that would give us cramps in our stomach.

There I'd be alright, bursting a gut to get outside and play with my pals. I was rightly locked down back then because my mother could hear the grass grow and she'd let a roar up the stairs if she heard me out of bed, *"I'm only going to do me poolie Ma'..."* I'd shout down to her as I made my way into our toilet. We didn't call it a bathroom back then; it was always the toilet or the older brothers used to say *"The Jacks"*. I was able to look out the little toilet window and see all the back gardens and some of the Oul Fellas digging and planting stuff to grow. Then I'd have to run and jump back into bed. Ah, they were hard times alright back then when I was sick and couldn't go out. So, I suppose now, like having the Flu, I just have to bide my time and eventually I'll be able to go out again. Now, let me see, where did I put them comics?

Story Twenty-Eight

Grandfather William Coffey

The Longers

Would young boys today know what is meant by *"Longers"?* Here's a photograph of my Grandad sitting down mending his shoe and wearing his Longers. When I was growing up it was only boys that were working who wore Longers. And they'd usually have a cigarette hanging out of the corner of their mouth like some gangster that you'd see on the big screen in the Picture House. I remember two of my older brothers having a row one time and one of them said to my mother, *"He's after thrunnin' me Longers under the bed and now they're all full of fluff and spiders"*. I think now they may have been a pair of *"Drain Pipes"* that he bought in Sloan's on Hire Purchase with his first week's wages from the Lemon's Sweet Factory in Drumcondra.

Your man from Sloan's, now, he wore Longers too because he was working, he would call to our house every Saturday morning for his money. He never knocked on the hall door or that, he'd just turn the key and walk in. We never took the key out of the door except at night when everyone was going to bed, some of our neighbours were posh and had their key on a piece of string and shoved in through the letterbox.

My father was always delighted to see your man from Sloan's because they'd spend the best part of an hour talking about football and Dalymount Park. He always made your man a fresh cup of tea and gave him a slice of toast, he was treated like some sort of long-lost relation.

When the older brother went working, he had to borrow a pair of my father's Longers because he didn't have a pair of his own and he had to hold them up with an *"S Belt"*. He had to turn the ends of the Longers up because they were miles too long on him and my mother held them in place by stitching them with thread. And there he was walking out the hall door throwing shapes because he was wearing Longers, I'm sure he thought he was John Wayne or some gangster or other.

I remember a time when my father's cousin sent out several oul pairs of Longers that he found in a bag in a lane somewhere off Moore Street. My mother cut the long legs off of them and sewed the remainder for us to wear as Shorts. The legs she cut off were used for dusting and cleaning, all very recyclable minded back then of course.

Nothing was ever thrown out of our house. Except the slop for the Pig Man who lived down the end of our road that is, he was Mister McKeever and he wore a cowboy hat and was as tall as Roy Rogers. I remember one of our neighbours asked me to bring a bucket of slop down to Mister McKeever and the bucket weighed a ton. I had to get me little pal, Willier Kavanagh, to help me with it. We had to stop every now and then because the handle of the bucket was tearing into our little hands and the slop was splashing out and running down our legs into our stockens. I'm glad that we weren't wearing Longers then or they'd have been destroyed with the smell of the slop.

We'd always knock on the door for Mister McKeever and he'd lift the heavy bucket up and empty everything into the great big metal barrel that he had for the slop. And some of it would splash back up and come flying out of the barrel and land in our hair. His wife always gave us a slice of bread and jam for being good boys.

My father used to fold the Longers from his good suit and place them under the mattress on his bed so they'd have a nice crease down the legs the next morning for when he was going to Mass. It took the brother a good while to get used to his Longers because he couldn't just run into the toilet anymore and do his Poolie like he used to by pulling up the leg of his shorts. No, he had to get used to opening the buttons in the fly and do it the way our father had to.

So now. I'm wondering if young lads these days would really know what I meant if they were asked what a pair of Longers was?

Story Twenty-Nine

My Sister's First Job

Here's a great little story that my sister told me recently about her first job. You see, one of her pals from our road went for a job interview when she was thirteen years old because she didn't fancy going back to school where the nuns were teaching. She had gone down to Blackhorse Place to a sewing factory where some other girls from Cabra were working.

My sister was also thirteen at this time but she loved school and wanted to stay on there. Now, what happened was this, her pal got the interview on a Friday and was supposed to start the following Monday but they told her she'd have to work a half day on a Saturday and of course back then it was never considered overtime or anything like that, it was just a normal part of your working week.

But on her way home the young one got the hump over this and when she got home, she told her mother about having to work on a Saturday and how she liked to stay in bed of a weekend. Her mother told her not to worry because she'd have a word with Misses Coffey down the road about it.

Well, there came this knock on our hall door and my mother told my sister to see who it was. In walks the oul one from up the road without a by your leave or anything to the sister and sits down at our kitchen table, where my mother is finishing off a cup of tea. *'Is there one in the pot...'* she says and pours herself out a cuppa. *"...I have something to ask you Misses Coffey"*.

Now my mother and herself were kind of pals as well as neighbours, do you know what I mean? They had moved into Cabra at about the same time during the war years or the *"Emergency"* as my father used to call it, so that's how they knew each other.

Anyway, she starts off telling my mother about her young one going for the job and her being kind of delicate and all that and how she loved staying in bed of a Saturday morning. *"Well..."* says my mother, looking over her glasses at the oul one, *"...what can I do about your young one because I know if it was one of mine she'd be out of bed before nine o'clock and helping me clean the house"*. The oul one put on this real Vincent de Paul face and reminds my mother that her young one is delicate and doesn't want the job and asks her if the sister could go down to the sewing factory and tell your man in charge. Now the sister is there cleaning the fender at the fireplace and ear-wiggin in on the conversation. Then the oul one says *"That's why I came down to you early you see, because the factory closes at twelve o'clock and I wanted to give your young one plenty of time to get down there"*.

So, off my sister goes out the hall door and she putting on her coat and scarf and of course she's muttering under her breath at how she'll reef the hair out of that young one the next time she sees her. Now it's a good walk from our house all the way down to Blackhorse Place, so it was a good thing that my sister was used to walking places with our mother. Sure, they used to walk all the way over to Meath Street every other Saturday for the shopping for our dinner on a Sunday. And then they'd walk home again after getting a cup of tea and maybe a plate of chips between them, with a bit of bread and butter each in a café in Thomas Street.

So, my sister finally arrives at the clothing factory and asks one of the young ones that she knew from Cabra who the manager was. Well out comes this big tall man and asks her what she wants. So, she ups and tells him the whole story about your one from up the road. Then when she finished talking to him, he says to her *"And what age are you then"*? She looked up at him and said *"I'm thirteen now and I'm still in school"*. *"Well..."* says he *"...then you can have your friend's job instead. You can start here on Monday morning at half past eight and don't be late. Oh, and bring your baptism certificate with you"*. And before she knew where she was, the poor sister had a job and she was so shocked that she hadn't time to tell your man that she didn't want it.

Anyway, she turned up on the Monday morning and began her working life in the Rag Trade. She eventually made a career of this and in later years opened up her own business in city centre which proved extremely successful. I think she stuck at it for at least sixty years. So, there you are and there you be, with that story of the sister and her first job.

The old Singer Sewing Machine

Story Thirty

The Road Lamp

Do you ever remember seeing the lamps like this by the side of the road when the Corporation would be laying down the Tar? They'd all be thrown in a heap by the side of the road until the watchman, *"The Gotchie"*, came on duty and he'd light each one up and place it along the road. They used to shine like little *"Red Eyed Devils"* at night. Me and the brother would be hiding behind the hedge in our garden looking out at them, afraid in case they saw us.

Then the Gotchie would sit down at his fire and he too would turn red from the light off the coke that he was burning. I used to love the smell from his fire. Sometimes he'd let the bigger lads toast bread on it and we'd be watching them. And he'd be puffing on a fag and coughing and spitting into the fire and all of a sudden this great big *"Hiss"* would roar out all over the place and he'd shout out, *"Get out you bastard"* and start laughing at the top of his voice and we'd see his gummy mouth go all red like the lamps on the road.

A man that lived near us had a bad chest and his wife used to ask the workmen for a bit of hot tar and they'd put it onto some brown paper that she'd have and when it was cool enough, she used to put it on her husband's chest. Other neighbours used to do it for a child with a bad cough, they'd get the child to inhale the fumes. We used to scrape the fresh tar with an ice pop stick and light them off the *"Gotchie's"* fire and we'd be running up and down the road pretending to be Indians setting fire to Fort Laramie.

One night some of the lads got over excited and set fire to a neighbour's hedge, it was great, the flames went shooting up into the air like they do on the Pictures and we were all whooping like Indians until the Oul Fella came out with a basin of water and threw it over us instead of over the blazing hedge.

We had gangs of kids on our road and in the Summer we'd all be allowed to stay out till real late and then when it was real dark, we'd play Kick the Can, *"You have to count up to a hundred in twos and then try to find us"*. My sister's loved playing Shop and we'd go rummaging in all the bins looking for broken delph to make the Chainie (Pretend money) with and to try and find empty tins and stuff. Our neighbour worked in Bachelors and she always had loads of oul tin cans in her bin.

My sister skipping with her pals

And the boys always came in handy when the girls were playing skipping with a double rope because the boys would turn the rope and all the girls would take turns running in and skipping, *"Look who's coming down the street, Mary O'Brien with Wah Wah feet, she was married seven times before and now she knocking at Christie Moran's door"*, and the laugh would be great if the lads roared out the wrong name of the boy whose door she was knocking on. I was never as good as the sister at Piggy Beds because I kept losing my balance and falling over.

Then my mother would be at the hall door shouting *"Come in, it's time for bed"* and then everyone would just disappear off the road, leaving the oul Gotchie on his own with his red lamps and coke fuelled fire and a bottle of Stout to keep him warm throughout the night, as we all cuddled up together, safe and warm, in our beds, dreaming of the Red Eyed Devils outside our window. For me, summer nights back then were always great because it stayed bright forever and ever and we went to bed tired from playing out all day long. And sometimes you couldn't wait to wake up in the morning to go out again and play some more.

My sister's and their dolls

Story Thirty-One

The School Inspector

I suppose the one day we all loved, besides our usual school holidays that is, in my class anyway, was the day that the School Inspector arrived. You see, some two or three weeks ahead of his arrival, our Teacher was always tipped off about his visit. He must have had a pal in the Department of Education or something that gave him the nod. Our Teacher would stand up in front of the classroom of forty young boys and holding the lapel of his coat in his left hand and his pipe in the other, he would announce, *"Now boys, it's that time of year again when our good friend, the School Inspector, will soon be calling in to see you all"*.

Now, if you were to be standing right there beside him you would have seen a tidal wave of grins of delight sweep right across our classroom. This was *"Show Time"* for us because almost immediately we'd go into rehearsals for his upcoming visit. Our Teacher always wanted to make sure that, besides us lads getting a good report from the Inspector, he too wanted nothing but good said about himself back to *"The Department"*.

Now, the layout of our classroom was quite interesting in that our Teacher was in some ways very much ahead of his time. In the first two rows of desks nearest to the door and the back half of the third row, sat all the boys that our Teacher considered brainy and quick on the uptake. The other two and a half rows were the boys who were a bit slower than the rest of us. Now, that wasn't a bad thing because the Teacher also split the Blackboard down the middle with a line of chalk, he was basically teaching two classes in one. There was never any fun made of a boy who might be a bit on the slow side and sometimes a faster boy might be put sitting beside him to help him out. Before I left this school, our Teacher had persuaded the Parish Priest to form a separate class for the *"Slow Learners"*, their classroom was upstairs and ours was downstairs.

All of us boys got on well together regardless of which side of the Blackboard we had to learn from.

And so, the rehearsals were quickly put in place. Certain boys were assigned to answer questions on Algebra, others on Irish and so on but I was always picked out to do the poem. There I'd be learning it off by heart in school, at home, in bed and even in my dreams. We all wanted to make a good impression on the oul Inspector because we knew that if we did there was always a reward to be had from our Teacher on that particular day.

I remember one time he had young Bernard Kelly practising his Irish Dancing out on the floor at the top of the class in order to impress the Inspector. It was all go; I can tell yeah. And even some of the slower boys were given assignments such as spelling or telling a little story about their family. Everything was in place to ensure that none of us failed to play our part.

For the next while we had very little in the way of lessons because they were only getting in the way of our upcoming *"Royal Command Performance"*. And then the day would arrive, it was always of a Friday after the ten o'clock Roll Call. Our Teacher would be there chomping on the stem of his oul pipe and pacing nervously across from one side of the classroom to the other in anticipation of our visitor. *"Now boys..."* he'd say *"...don't let me down, I'm depending on you all to make a good impression today"*.

And then there it would be, a rap tap tap on our classroom door. Be the jakers our little hearts would be jumping inside our chests with the fright of the knock. The poor oul Teacher would nearly have a heart attack and the tobacco from this pipe would be spluttering all over the classroom as he too jumped up with fright. Just before he'd open the door, he'd give one last look at us young lads and we knew from that look not to let him down or else. He'd pull open the door with a great big swish and a broad smile across his face as he reached out to shake the Inspector's hand.

Mitching from School

"Curtain up, light the lights, we've got nothing to fear but the heights...", the show was on the road. The Inspector would step in and rubbing his little moustache he'd say *"Dia dhuit boys"* and we'd all have to answer him with, *"Dias Muire dhuit"*. The Inspector would sit down on our Teacher's chair and taking a pen from his top pocket and putting on his brown horn rimmed glasses, he would check the Roll Book to see that it was being marked correctly, he always did that first and of course on that particular day we would have a full attendance in class because we would have received a very real threat from the Teacher if any of us were missing on that day.

Now, when the Inspector would ask a question of the boys, he always left it up to our Teacher to pick out who would answer. The Inspector would look out over the classroom and say, *"I have ten oranges in one box and ten oranges in another box. If I eat two oranges out of the first box and eat four oranges out of the second box, how many oranges will I have left"*?

Straightaway the few boys that our Teacher already had primed would shoot their hands up into the air *"Sir, sir"* they'd call out, all excited to give the correct answer. Eventually it would come to the point where the Inspector would ask *"Is there any boy who would like to recite a poem for me"*? One boy over near the window would put his hand halfway up and pretend he wanted to but I'd be shooting my hand up as far as I could and the Teacher would pick me. I'd stand out beside my desk and start off at the top of my voice, *"I think that I shall never see, a poem lovely as a tree. A tree that looks at God all day and lifts her leafy arms to pray..."* and on I'd go until finally *"...Poems are made by fools like me but only God can make a tree".* Our Teacher would give me a wink and a little nod of approval and then I'd sit down.

The Inspector would then have a few words in private with our Teacher, they'd be after whispering to each other, and then our Teacher would turn to the class and say *"Now boys, the School Inspector is very impressed by you all here today and suggested that I give you no Homework for the weekend".* We'd give out a big cheer of thanks and off the Inspector would go. Our poor Teacher would take a hanky out of his pocket and wiping the sweat off his brow, would plonk himself down into his chair with a great big sigh of relief.

So that would bring us up near to lunch time and we'd all be sitting there with abated breath as the Teacher would look down at us as he lit his pipe, he'd have a twinkle in his eye and say, *"I think you all deserve a half day off today boys, well done and off you go now but quietly, we don't want the whole school to know".*

We'd all sneak out the side door of the school and as soon as we were outside the gate, we'd give a great big cheer and scatter off home. And there'd be our Teacher cycling off to the pub for a few pints and singing at the top of his voice, knowing that the Department of Education was going to get a glowing report on him and his boys.

Story Thirty-Two

Mr Byrne, my School Teacher

To Sir with Love

I remember as a young fella when I'd be up at the crack of dawn and bursting a gut to get out to school. My mother was always first to get up out of bed in our house and she'd go downstairs to put the kettle on for my father's cup of tea before he'd head off to work. Looking back now I think that maybe there was something wrong with me because I loved going to school and couldn't wait to get to my classroom. Some of my little pals were nearly just as bad because they'd be knocking on our hall door about a half an hour before the brothers or anyone else went to school. This was especially so when we became big lads and were going to the all-boys National School in Cabra West where we had a man as a teacher and not a nun. Now, we all loved our nun, Sister Mary Oliver, she was a very gentle and mammy sort of nun.

THE SCHOOL MASTER

There were forty boys in my class in school

But do you know what? There was nothing quite as adventurous as going to the Big School. Well, I know that our new classroom was not as clean or polished as the convent school, it looked a bit rough and ready and it didn't have fresh flowers on the window sill either but I loved it just the same. I remember that most of the nuns were very quiet in their manner and almost glided along the corridors but in the Big School you could hear the Master's roaring and shouting all over the place. There might be some poor young fella being dragged along the corridor by the ear and his Master lashing him across the back of the legs with a cane. Or we might have the father of some other young fella having a punch up with one of the Masters. There was always great excitement when we'd see someone's Da' marching into the school because we'd hear great stories then when we were out in the schoolyard at lunch time.

Now, rough and ready as this school was, I was extremely fortunate to have the Master I had, Mister Byrne. He was Dublin born and reared. He told us that his father had worked all his life as a Milkman and delivered milk to houses and cottages up in the mountains.

I remember one day he brought our whole class of 40 boys upstairs in the school so that we could look out the window and he could point out the Dublin Mountains a million miles away out in the country, well that's what it seemed like to us, we never knew that life existed south of O'Connell Bridge or further up the Navan Road past Ashtown. Mister Byrne told us that the Phoenix Park was his playground when he was a boy. Over the years he would tell us many stories about his parents and his younger life. The one thing that always reminds me of him is the smell of tobacco from a pipe.

Anytime that he was going to tell us a story he'd say to the two boys sitting in the desk at the front of the class *"Move over there boys"* and he'd sit up on the desk with his feet on the seat. He'd take his pipe out of his top pocket and light it up and after a couple of puffs or so he'd start off with some story or other. Sometimes he'd bring in a musical instrument in a long wooden case like a clarinet type of thing. Some of the boys used to call it *"His Flute"* but they didn't mean that in a musical sort of way.

Our Master was a great lover of all things Irish and especially music and dance. He'd play some of the most beautiful tunes we'd ever heard and sometimes we'd see him nearly crying. He taught us how to play the Tin Whistle. Most every day when we were brought to the toilet after the ten o'clock Roll Call, he'd show us how to do some Irish dance or other. I was useless with my two left feet but one boy named Bernard Kelly was very good at it. Mister Byrne was a well-known traditional Irish musician and appeared on Telefis Eireann a few times doing his dancing.

Now, I did get my fair share of slaps from his cane and only once do I remember him losing his temper in class. When we'd be getting a slap and we'd be tempted to pull our hand back he'd snarl at us and if he had the pipe in his mouth the ash from it went all over the place.

What I used to love most about school was the Roll Call at ten o'clock because there were always a few boys on the mitch. I always got the job of going to their mother for a note, which I always wrote because most of the mammies could barely read or write. And for this the boys had to pay me with sweets afterwards.

We used to love it when our school holidays were over because the Master would tell us all about his own holidays over in

Connemara and the cottage he stayed in with his young family. I remember when he was teaching us the poem called *"The Old Woman of the Road"* and he drew a picture on the blackboard of his holiday cottage.

In later years, while my youngest brother was still attending this school, the Da' went to a parent's meeting and my oul teacher came over to the Da' and asked about me and how I was doing. A while later I called to the school to see him and he brought me into his classroom, it was like stepping back in time, nothing had changed. He had me speak to the boys about my time in school and then he brought me down to the Teacher's Room for a cuppa tea. I knew then that I had grown up because I was only ever in that room when I had to get his cup of tea when I was ten years old.

I really enjoyed that visit and my time with him, even though it did seem strange talking to my Master on a one to one level. I never disliked or hated my teacher; he had a great influence for the good on my younger life. I feel sad that most of my older brothers never had this relationship with the teachers they had over the years in the same school. I have heard so many horror stories from them and their pals about the physical abuse they received and leaving school with little or no education. I was nearly crying when I had to leave my Master and go to the Tech. To me he was a great man and a great teacher and I've never forgotten that and even when I meet some of my old school pals, they all say the same. Thank you, sir.

Off to School

The Cabra Baths 1940's.

Story Thirty-Three

Willie Kavanagh and Martin Coffey

My Best Pal

This little story is based on a recollection of what I think I can remember of my childhood and what I was later told by my mother. Because there were fifteen of us at home some of what I remember of my life as a young boy may actually consist of a mixture of many stories and events that had happened to not only me but to my brothers and sisters, in our house over those years.

A little bit like my mother when she'd be baking a cake for our Sunday Tea, she would throw in a little bit of this and that, a handful here and there, no fancy measuring spoons or weighing scales involved, just whatever she felt like at the time. And I suppose that's what my stories are like in content, a little pinch of salt from the brothers or handful of flour from the older sisters, mix it all up and like the Christmas Pudding, make a wish and out of the oven of life comes a story of how I remember things to have been.

On this particular occasion I was talking to my mother about the day I first started in school, I was four years old. And there was my little pal, Willier Kavanagh, we were almost like twins, you never saw one without the other tagging along. I remember him and I walking up our road that morning and we holding each other's hand, the excitement was electric, we were going to school and that made us *"Big Boy's"* now.

This was the beginning of a great big adventure for the both of us, just like the first day we went to the Pictures to see our very first Cowboy film, never again would life be what it had been for us two little fellas. I can see us now, strutting up the road holding hands and the two Ma's walking behind us, yakking away to each other and of course some of the older brothers would have been galloping ahead of us because they already knew where to go.

My mother told me that when we arrived up at the school there was a queue the Mammy's had to stand in with their little new beginners. She said there were two Nun's at the top of the queue, one was sitting at a table taking down names and so on and another one standing next to her with a leather strap in her hand. My mother said she felt like she was back in school herself and was afraid to make a sound in case she got a slap of the leather. Now, myself and Willier were still holding hands but our grip had gotten a little tighter as we came to realise that the two Ma's were going to leave us here in this strange place.

When we reached the top of the queue my mother had to give my name to the Nun and I was told to *"Go in there"* and so I went to do just that but I was still gripping on to my little pal's hand and he on to mine. As he moved in the same direction as me the Nun let out a roar at him to stay where he was. I can tell you now that the whole queue leaped three feet into the air with the fright. Poor little Willier started crying *"Ma' I want to go in with Martin, I'm afraid on me own"*. So, we now had a stand-off between the two Nun's and the two Ma's. It came down to a staring competition but the Nun's hadn't a hope in Hell of getting the better of the two Ma's and so after what seemed like a million years, Willier was let follow me into the classroom. The Nuns were bulling, or so my mother said.

And so, it was that way for the next eight or nine years, us two little fellas went to school with each other every day, hail, rain or snow. And when the school bell rang, we'd gallop out together and we'd keep running until we reached our garden gates and home. The dinner was gulped down as fast as we could because we wanted to get out and head up to the Phoenix Park or down to the Cattle

Market on another one of our adventures together. We even made our First Holy Communion together and our Confirmation as well.

As we hit our late teens our road of life split in two and we headed off in whatever direction life took us. But over the years we'd often bump into each other and even up to recent times we were just the same, sharing a laugh and a joke and remembering some mischief we got up to as little fellas. I suppose the only real harm we ever did as young fellas was robbing some orchard or other or sneaking into the grounds of the Christian Brothers' place and stealing their Rhubarb.

Willier's mother died shortly after we had started school and I remember many the time he'd be sitting next to me at our dinner table having a bite to eat with the rest of us. In very recent years Willier joined his Ma' in Heaven and I remember sitting in the church at his funeral with all these types of stories running wild inside my head and shedding a little tear at the loss of my pal. So now, there you have it, I hope you enjoyed that little ramble with meself and Willier.

Story Thirty-Four

The Slide

I remember after school one day, in the middle of a very frosty winter, a gang of young lads got an old sack and dipped it down a shore by the side of the road to get it good and wet. Then they slapped it down onto the footpath outside our house and covered the path in water. About an hour later the water had turned into ice and made a great slide for us all to play on. If any of the old people came along, we'd tell them to walk on the road in case they slipped on the ice. A gang of kids, boys and girls of all ages, would form a big queue and we'd all take our turn in having a slide. It was always great fun and there'd be lots of laughter when anyone would slip and fall. When it came my turn however, I was about halfway along the slide, when I went on my ear. As I was falling, I remember the shouts of laughter from my pals and then I felt a great big bang at the back of my head, then everything went black.

I woke up sometime later lying on the floor in our kitchen beside the fire, I'd been knocked unconscious by the fall. My head felt very sore and I was dizzy if I stood up. My mother said I wasn't to be going on them slides anymore or I might end up in hospital.

Some of my pals knocked on our hall door and asked if I was alright and if I was coming back out to play on the slide. My mother let me sit in our parlour and look out the window at all the fun my pals were having on the slide but I was under her strict orders not to try and sneak out or else.

And that was always the threat, *"Or else"*. That could mean anything from getting a hiding to being sent up to bed early or not getting any tea. It could even mean she'd tell my father on you and that was even worse than any of the other threats but I don't think she ever did because when he would come home from work on his bike he'd be freezing cold like the slide outside our house and he'd just want his dinner and a cup of tea. You could always feel the cold off him when he'd be taking his bicycle out through our kitchen to his shed out the back.

But somehow or other us kids never seemed to have felt the cold when we were outdoors in the winter. We'd always be doing something to keep ourselves warm and active. Of course, there was always the slide. We'd go up along the canal and try to break the ice on top of the water by throwing great big rocks off the bridge onto the ice below. The rocks would make a great big bang sound and slide over the ice if it didn't break it. And sometimes we'd throw a stick out onto the ice for one of our dogs to fetch and we'd have a great laugh at the dog slip sliding all over the place and then he'd come out but would never go back in, smart dog or what!!! We had great times in the winter back then and always loved coming home to a nice warm fire and our tea at six o'clock.

North Cumberland Street Market

Story Thirty-Five

My father with L_R: Brendan, Anne, Martin sitting on the
ground, Noel and my cousin, John Burke

The Carnival

Do you ever remember the excitement when a Carnival came to the
area? We'd always go up straight after school and ramble around
the outside trying to see all the things. They'd have a Cliff Richard
song blaring out all over the place. We'd be shouting in over the

fence *"Hey Mister, gis a job"* and trying to figure out some way or other of bunking in for free. I remember seeing a film one time about a young boy who ran away with the circus and I always thought that's what I'm going to do some day. Can you imagine the excitement of it, there'd I'd be, at the end of the day, heading off into the setting sun like the Chap on his horse at the Pictures.

I used to love the *"Shooting Gallery* "with the pellet rifles and even though we were only about three or four feet away from the target we still managed to miss it because your man would tell you to look down the sights and then shoot but the whole thing was a scam, the sights were as crooked as a bent penny. And then there was the stall where you threw three darts at the ace of spades or some target or other and if the dart stuck in them then you won a prize. The catch there was that the tips on the darts were as blunt as me boots and wouldn't stick in butter.

And here, what about throwing the three rubber rings at the board? That would work great if the board was up straight but it was always at an angle so that one side of the ring would hit the board and throw everything off kilter. Then you had the plastic yellow ducks floating around in a circle and you'd have to hook one up with a stick and if the duck had a ticket stuck underneath, you'd win a prize. You'd be delighted but the prize was always some cheap oul toy like something out of Hector Grey's shop but it didn't matter, you'd won the prize.

I remember in the mid 1960's going to a carnival in a place at the far side of Phibsborough church. It was the only time I ever saw the

Wall of Death in action. It was just like Elvis Presley in Roustabout with the noise of the motorbike engines being revved and the smell of petrol fumes filling the air. There'd be these two fellas sitting on the same motorbike and they start off real sort of slow and then the bike would rev up and they'd take off, swoosh and up they'd come, speeding around the wall of death.

And all the girls standing around would let out a great big scream pretending they were scared. I think they only did that so the fellas on the bike would look at them and give them the eye. Me and the pals would love to be doing that motorbike thing and have all the girls screaming at us. I wonder whatever became of those wall of death lads and where they are now. They're all probably on the old age pension or something. Do they ever tell their grandchildren about the Wall of Death?

And then there was the Fortune Teller's tent, Madam Gazeebo. Get your palms red for three pence and see what the future holds. Young courting couples going in to see when would they get married and how many kids would they have. And other couples wanting to know what was their chances of getting a house in the *"Newly Weds Draw"*. Then there was always the lads going in to see which Moth should they ask out and if she would say yes or no. It was great fun altogether and harmless oul stuff.

The Bumpers were always a great attraction at any carnival. I think they were my favourite. The lads would always try and convince some Young One to let them sit in it with them. *'I know how to drive, sure haven't I got a bike'.*

The crack would be ninety and the roars and screams every time someone crashed into the back of someone else's bumper car. The ould fella in charge was always shouting *'No crashing allowed, you all have to go the one way'*. Sure, whoever listened to him anyway and there he'd be standing on the back of a car and holding onto the bar with one hand and rattling the money in the other to remind you to pay up.

But we all loved the good oul Bumpers, especially at night when it got dark and the sparks they gave off from the overhead wires made it all the more exciting. What a great time we had back then, just good clean fun at the Carnival.

Girl's playing Piggy Beds

Story Thirty-Six

Our Comic Cuts

These few Comics are just a very small selection of all the Comic Cuts that used to be out when I was a young boy. There were more comics for sale in the shops back then than there were newspapers. I remember one day in 1961 when I went to buy a Comic with that date, 1961 on it, because if you turned the date upside down it would still read the same and every one of my pals thought that was such a great thing to be able to do. Now, that Comic then was priced on the front cover as threepence or thruppence, depending on how you said it and I handed Your One behind the counter, the one with the long face, the money and she told me I had to pay sixpence, She said it was only people in England that got it for threepence but we had to pay more.

I remember putting my Trupenny Bit on the counter and suddenly making a mad dash out of the shop with the Comic in my hand. I was like a Greyhound then; a little skinny thing and she couldn't chase after me anyway because she was the only one working behind the counter. I think it was a copy of the Beano or the Dandy that I made off with.

I remember when the sister, who was a nurse in England, used to send home boxes of clothes belonging to patients that had died in the hospital where she worked and sometimes, she'd include a load of old comics for us. Some of the more popular comics in my time were the Beano, the Dandy, the Judy and the Bunty, most everyone looked at these, both boys and girls.

Then, depending on your taste, there was the Hotspur, the Eagle, the Victor, the Topper, the Sparky, the Whizzer, the Jack and Jill, the Beezer, the Buster, the Diana, the Marvel Comics, the Commando 64rs, the Wham, the Knockout, the Rover, the Valiant, the Hurricane, the Jackie, the Mandy, the School Friends and probably many more that I can't remember. The great thing about the comics was that you didn't even have to know how to read because of the pictures and drawings inside, you could just let your imagination take over and away you went.

Me reading a Comic in our toilet

I always remember of a winter's night going around our road with the brother looking for *"Swaps"* from other boys. That meant exchanging some of our comics for some of theirs and haggling for a bargain if you had an American comic, which might be worth two or three ordinary comics. Or sometimes if the other fella had comics that were a bit torn and worn down to a few scraps of paper, well then you could easily get a good swap.

Now, the boy's 64rs, small war comics, were worth three or maybe four other comics, depending on their condition and if you wanted it bad enough. Sometimes we'd go out for swaps with loads of comics under our arms and come home with just a few new ones but it was always worth it and especially if we got something that very few other boys would have. We'd be let sit in on the bottom of their stairs out of the rain and the cold to do our business.

Sometimes one of your man's sisters might come out and ask us if we had any Bunty's or Judy's or any girl's comics. The brother used to say that they only came out to have a look at us, now what did that mean to me at the time? I was only interested in swapping comics, not swapping spits and kisses, after all you can't hide under the bedcovers with them and your torch to have a good read.

Myself and the brother would be bursting to get home then and settle down for the night by our fireplace and have a browse through all our swaps. The sister said she used to do all her swaps in school but if the Nun's saw her doing it, she was in trouble. Although there seemed to be a lot of violence in some of the comics, that didn't necessarily influence the way we behaved. Somehow or other that type of entertainment never crossed the line and I suppose in some way our parents saw to that.

The comics, for me, were pure fantasy and escapism, a great laugh to be enjoyed but not copied and especially where the Dennis the Menace or the Bash Street Kids were involved because we were never bullies to other boys nor them to us, there would be the odd disagreement or a scrap maybe, but nothing so violent as to put someone into hospital, because we saw it in a comic.

We used to get hours of fun from our comics and the sister's cutting out the doll shapes with their outfits from the back page of their comic. If any of us were ever sick in bed the Da' would bring us home a new comic of a Friday when he came home from work. We'd be sitting up in bed reading the comic and drinking a sup of Lucozade and that always made us feel so much better.

I went out recently to buy two comics for little pals of mine but the shop had none, anything that was there was only over-priced rubbish that you'd never get swaps for in my day. It's such a sad thing that these comics are no longer being printed. What a great loss to the generations coming after us. But maybe someday things will take a turn around and we'll see a revival for the comic and the mobile phones being left to one side while the younger ones sit down and have a good read and a laugh.

Story Thirty-Seven

The Wedding 1963

I remember the time my sister Chrissie got married to Tony Duffy, because I wasn't at that wedding, I was the only one in our family who didn't attend it. Not because I didn't want to that is, but because I ended up in hospital the night before with a threatened burst appendix. Some days or so before the wedding my mother had me bring her coat and a few other pieces to the Dry Cleaners so that they would look like new on the big day.

I remember the morning before the wedding being in a lot of pain when I woke up. My brother said it was probably just stomach cramps from eating a sour apple or something. As the day wore on, I was becoming worse. I said it to my mother and it was then she remembered that the   dry cleaning had to be collected. So off I was sent with our baby's pushchair to bring the clothes home in. I remember feeling dizzy and very hot. As I walked along I could feel beads of sweat dripping down my face.

When I finally reached the Dry Cleaners the girl there told me that the items weren't quite ready and would take about another half hour or so. I remember waiting outside the shop door and everything was spinning around, so I sat in the baby pushchair. I must have fallen asleep because the girl from the Cleaners came out and woke me up. I could hardly stand up and wasn't sure if I was going to make it back home or not.

That journey seemed never ending, the road was endless and my head was throbbing with the pain. I remember stopping at one point and getting sick, I knew then that I wasn't well and needed to get home double quick. The next thing I remember is being in bed and my mother standing over me with a worried look on her face. I know I couldn't sit up and was barely able to talk. Lucky for me one of our neighbours was passing me by when I collapsed onto the path and fell unconscious.

The neighbour stopped a car and that's how I ended up in bed. Our house was a hive of activity in preparation for the wedding the next morning but I wasn't able to be a part of it. My eldest sister and her husband were due home from England for the wedding and they were to sleep on the bed-settee in our front parlour. It was all hands-on deck, polishing shoes, ironing shirts and hair curlers in place. I was in and out of sleep for most of the time, I had little or no idea where I was or what day it was. When my sister from

England arrived in the door my father told her about me. She was a trained nurse and immediately went into action. I remember her sitting on the edge of my bed and taking my temperature she told my father to send for a doctor straightaway, it looked like I had appendicitis.

When the doctor arrived, my parents were told that I would have to go straight to hospital as I had a threatened burst appendix. As if my poor parents didn't have enough on their plate in trying to organise everyone and everything for the forthcoming wedding, they now had this to contend with. My father ran around to the nearest phone box and rang for a taxi to take me to hospital.

When the driver arrived, he was about to take us to Temple Street Hospital but the doctor told him to take me to Crumlin Hospital, she said she would ring ahead and let them know. I remember my father coming into the bedroom and telling me that I had to go to hospital. He then wrapped me in a blanket, lifted me up in his arms and brought me down to the waiting taxi.

My sister accompanied us to the hospital. I remember that night, lying in bed and looking out the window across the hospital grounds at a building with flashing neon lights. I later found out it was the Star Cinema across the road. I of course had no idea where I was, I just remember the taxi journey seemed to go on forever. At that stage of my life I had never been that far south of the River Liffey. And so, I remained a patient here for three or four days, having missed my sister's wedding and of course, a piece of her wedding cake too.

Story Thirty-Eight

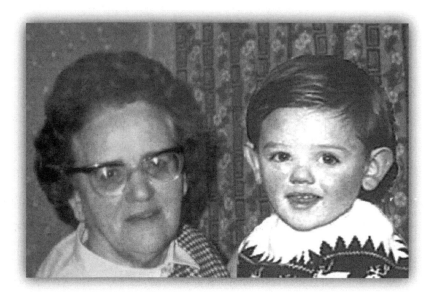

The Mammy with Joe Coffey

What's Your Name?

I always remember that my mother would never leave our house without her scarf on and a little bit of lipstick, even if she was only going up to the local shops for a loaf of bread and a half pound of Margarine. With the gang of us in the house it was a constant battle to keep it clean and tidy but somehow or other she managed to whip us all into shape and gave each of us a job to do in keeping it clean.

Every morning after we had all gone to school, she would make all the beds, tidy the kitchen and go to the shops for the day's food and dinner. Like my father, she never stopped going. But they were no different than most of our neighbours back then, big families were all the go in those days and parents seldom got a minute to themselves. Our dinner was served up when we came home from school, our tea was at six o'clock and we were off to bed by nine o'clock.

My Mother was born in the Rotunda Hospital in 1919, her mother lived in 20 Railway Street, in the Monto. She was registered by the hospital under the name of Mary Carroll, the name her mother gave. Her mother's pal took her to the church to be baptised and she was mistakenly christened under the name of Mary Agnes Spellman, when she was two years old her mother married John Burke and so my mother then became known as Aggie Burke. When she married my father in 1938, she was asked by the Priest to produce a copy of her baptism certificate, she then became Aggie Coffey.

Every one of her children have our mother's name on their birth certificates as Mary Agnes Spellman. This has caused more confusion in our family because whenever we were asked by some government official or other what our mother's maiden name was, we'd always say, Carroll or some of us would say Spellman and then there were even some of us who would say Burke.

I remember the time in recent years when I took her for an eye test and the receptionist called out *"Mary Coffey next"*, the Ma' stood up and walked towards her. I said *"It's not you Ma' it's a Mary Coffey, you're Aggie'*. She looked at me with a great big grin on her face and kept walking to the eye test room. Later on, I asked her about this and she told me that her real name is Mary and not

Aggie, even though everyone, including her siblings and her mother, called her Aggie.

My mother told me that she had a very happy upbringing regardless of the poverty by which she was surrounded. She had lots of friends who, like herself, never knew their birth father. She told me that her stepfather was better than any father she could have ever asked for, she always had a great love and respect for him and he for her. She told me that there were a lot of the local women who she called her Aunts but they were actually not related, she later referred to them as *"The Girls"*, meaning that they had to earn a living on the streets. She would sometimes help them out by going to the shops for cigarettes and bottles of Porter whenever a man was calling. Other times she would clean their rooms out for them. Sometimes, my mother would sleep in a great big old iron and brass bed with at least six other children belonging to *"The Girls"*, she said it never mattered whether they were boys or girls because they were only kids.

Her mother had two more children, one of whom died a few days after her fourth birthday. And I should mention that she had an older brother, Johnnie Carroll, who she loved to bits, he was a real big brother to her. She said that it broke her heart when her stepfather died in 1927. He was offloading a consignment of wheat from a boat on the docks, the S.S. Londonderry, when he collapsed and died. The dust from the wheat had clogged up his airways, as he struggled to get his breath, he took a heart attack. My mother's

"Auntie Mary" who wasn't her Auntie, taught her how to read and write before she was of school age.

Life for my parents was a constant struggle and one of survival against all of the odds that was thrown at them over the years. With so many children in the one house there was always at least one of us sick, at the doctor or in hospital. My mother helped to lay out the dead, deliver babies and wiped many a snotty nose belonging to kids in the area.

In more recent times she told me that she often cried herself to sleep longing for her mother. When my father passed away, she also missed him something terrible. If she heard a good joke at her Bingo she'd go home and sitting on the bed, she'd say to the Da', *"Are you listening"? I have another joke for you"*. And off she'd go with it and then cry herself to sleep because she missed him so much. There was never a time that they didn't know each other, he remembered the day she was brought home from the Rotunda as a baby, he was five years old.

Story Thirty-Nine

The Sunshine House

I remember the first time I ever left home to go away on holiday by myself. I didn't know it was a holiday of course because nobody ever told me. I clearly remember one night in particular when my father arrived home from work on his bike. He always seemed to get home at around six o'clock every evening and as soon as my mother would hear the Angelus Bells ringing out from our local church she'd say *"Your Daddy will be in any minute now, pour the tea"*, and as sure as not he'd walk in the door pushing his bike through the kitchen and out to his shed. He cycled through hail, rain and snow to and from work every day. He worked in the Bank as a

Porter and every year he would get a new suit made, paid for by the Bank of course, and a new woollen overcoat every three years.

Well this particular evening as my father was lapping up his plate of stew, he told me to go upstairs and wash my face and hands because he was going to bring me out on his bike when he'd finished his dinner. So, off I went and did as I was told, as we did then, without question. Well in next to no time at all I was sitting on the crossbar of his bike and heading off in towards town. I was enjoying the trip as my father would always be singing and whistling as he pedalled along. We eventually came to a very big house, well it looked like one of them tenement houses that my father's cousin lived in, and it was across the road from a park, I later found out it was Mountjoy Square. It was a big house and when we climbed what seemed like a hundred stairs, we went in to a room where a Doctor was waiting to examine me. Now, at this point I had no idea what this was all about but I just did what my father told me to do. The Doctor did his thing by listening to my chest but never said a word and meself and the Da' were heading home in next to no time at all.

Now, a couple of weeks later, on a Saturday morning, my father told me to get dressed because he was bringing me into town, and so I did. This time we came to Amiens Street train station. There was a great big group of young boys, all around my own age, standing up near the platform. My father told me to go and stand with the boys and so I did. He pedalled away off home and left me standing there, I had no idea what was going on or why he left me there. A rough looking boy asked me my name and told me we were going down to the country on a train. Then, all of a sudden, the penny dropped, I was being sent away to a boy's orphanage down the country, but why, what did I do wrong on my mother, I was nearly always good in school. So, eventually the bunch of us lads were marched further up the platform where we boarded a train for the country. Most of the other young boys were delighted and excitedly talking about Balbriggan, wherever that was I didn't know.

And so, it was that I ended up in the Sunshine House in Balbriggan for a week's holiday. I became pals with a young boy named Billy Pidgeon, he was great because he seemed to know the ropes and told me not to worry and not to be crying. I was delighted when my new pal told me that we'd be going back home at the end of the week, I wasn't being left in an orphanage after all. At home, I shared a bed with two of my brothers and I never had a bed to myself until I went to the Sunshine House. I had a great time in Balbriggan playing games and going down to the beach where we were given little black swimming shorts to wear. Most nights we had a film show and on the last night of our holiday there was a concert. I got up on the small stage and sang *"Old McDonald had a farm"* and I won a prize for it. I couldn't wait to get home to show the Ma' what I had won.

I remember one night when it was dark, the Leaders took us for a walk to a graveyard. We were told that a man by the name of McKenzie was buried there and that every night he haunted the

Sunshine House and especially the toilets. I later reckoned that was a way to stop us running in and out to the toilet all night. We were all told to sit down on the ground in the middle of all the graves while we were told a Ghost Story.

I was sitting next to Billy Pigeon and we were nearly crying and shaking with the fright, we had to hold each other's hand to make sure that the ghost didn't take one of us away. Billy told me to say a Hail Mary before I got into bed and that way the ghost wouldn't go near me. I knew he must be right because he had been here before and that's what he must have done as well. And, do you know what? The very next morning when we woke up there was one of the beds in our dormitory sitting up on top of another bed, we couldn't believe it. The Leaders told us it must have been McKenzie's Ghost that put it there. Meself and Billy were gobsmacked at the notion that the ghost actually came into our dormitory and we never even knew.

And so, the following Saturday came along all too quickly, it was time to go home. It was very sad really because some of the young boys were actually crying and wanted to stay another week, they had such a great time of it. I remember meself and Billy sitting together in the train watching all the green fields and the cows going by faster and faster as the train picked up speed. And we could even see the beach where we made sandcastles together. So, that was my first ever holiday away from home, a week in the Sunshine House in Balbriggan.

Sunshine Boys 1960's

Wash Time

Girl's week in the Sunshine House.

Story Forty

My Old Guitar

In 1963 my older brother Brendan got a guitar for Christmas. This was the first time I had ever seen a real guitar up close. Nobody in our house knew the first thing about guitars, they didn't know that a guitar had to be tuned to a certain setting or how to strum it correctly. Brendan's guitar usually lay on the floor underneath our bed, gathering dust. Sometimes and especially after school I would go to the bedroom and take up the guitar to see if I could figure out how to play it. One day, by sheer fluke, I figured out how to place one finger on the bottom string and by moving it left or right while plucking the string, I could make a musical sound. This was my moment of introduction to the world of music; I had cracked the code and opened a door into another dimension where I became well and truely hooked. I was then able to put one note to another and make a little tune out of them. At first Brendan wasn't too pleased with me for being at his guitar but over time he relented.

One evening I was walking home from some place or other when I came upon a small group of older lads playing guitars at the top of our road. One of them was Kevin Kennerney and another was Jimmy Marshall, both of whom went on to carve out very successful musical careers for themselves. I remember telling Kevin that I could play a song on the guitar. Now, to put things into perspective, guitar players are very territorial when it comes to letting someone else play their guitar, so, he sent me home to get my guitar or should I say Brendan's guitar. I soon enough arrived back to the group and played my one string tune for them. They were so impressed that they all laughed out loud and in harmony with each other, I was delighted at such a response and took it that I was now one of their guitar gang. But not so, I had to serve my apprenticeship first. This came in the shape of something the lads called *"Chords"*. First off, they tuned Brendan's guitar and warned me not to let anyone touch the tuning pegs, secondly, I had to practice my first chord until it was note perfect, then and only then could I come back to the gang. So off home with myself I headed, I had a few new words in my vocabulary, Chords, Frets and Tuning.

Now, I have to say that Brendan's guitar strings were far too high up off the fretboard, that's what the lads called the neck of the guitar, and being made of steel, they cut a groove into the tips of each of the fingers on my left hand. As a result of which I would bleed and watch the skin peel off the tips of my fingers. I never knew then of nylon guitar strings; they were to come much later. But I persevered and eventually got the nack of how to hold down my first guitar chord, the chord of D Major. I used to drive everyone in our house mad from playing the same thing over and over. As soon as I'd arrive home from school, I'd gulp down my dinner, do my ecker (Homework) and gallop upstairs to the guitar. And that's where I would stay for hour after hour practising and putting up with the pain in my fingertips until eventually, I felt confident enough to go back up the road to the guitar gang standing on the corner.

I was then shown a second and third chord and eventually introduced to how to play a song by using these three chords. It really didn't take me too long before I felt confident enough to stand in front of my parents and play a song for them, *"You are my sunshine"*. I didn't know all of the words of course but they didn't mind, my father knew more than I did, we had great craic. And that was my first live performance playing the guitar. The lads on the corner then showed me a few more chords and told me what songs to sing with them, these fellas were great, they had the patients of all the Saints in Heaven.

They would even get me to sing with them, these fellas were great. I remember watching them playing and singing and I couldn't believe the talent that each of them had. My poor little head would be buzzing from all that they showed me and from the songs they would sing.

When I was fourteen years old, I decided I wanted to buy myself a new guitar. Now, the only money I had back then was two shillings and six pence or half a dollar as we used to call it, "*Pocket Money*" that the Da' would give me of a Friday night and the shilling the Ma' would give me for collecting the welfare milk for her every morning before I went to school. She was entitled to two bottles of free milk a day and they had to be collected from a house not too far from where we lived. Now, my brother Brendan had started work and had joined the newly opened Credit Union in our area, so I asked him to borrow some money for me and I would pay him back every Friday and he could in turn pay off the Credit Union. I had seen a guitar with nylon strings on it in the window of Clerys in O'Connell Street for five pounds and I decided to get that one. So, Brendan took out the loan from the Credit Union and I paid him the half dollar that I got from my father, so I suppose you could say that the Da' bought me my first guitar.

I remember when I was about fourteen years old, one evening I was sitting at our table looking through the newspaper for the cartoons when I spotted a letter to the Editor from a Variety Group looking for musicians of all kinds, to go out and entertain people in hospitals, schools, concert halls and orphanages. I showed it to my

Da' and he there and then handed me a blank page and a pencil and told me to write in to them.

I received a letter back inviting me to an audition. It was held in a big house on Parnell Square. I remember I was shaking at the idea of getting up and playing in front of all the people who I didn't know. Your man in charge had to call my name out twice because I was so nervous, I didn't hear him the first time. I stood up by the piano and did my piece, one song and then sat down and that was it, over and done with in seconds, although it did seem like I was up for ages.

Then a young lad stood up and played on his Tin Whistle, next came a group of young lads singing ballads, they were called the Cooley Folk. Two young ones, sisters, stood up and did a clown act and so it went for the rest of the night. Then I headed home on the bus not knowing if I had been selected or not.

The following day a woman called to our house and told my mother that I had been successfully chosen to be a part of the Variety Group. Everyone chosen was to meet up the following Sunday in Parnell Square at one o'clock because we were all going to a hospital in Dunlaoghaire to entertain the patients there. Little did I know then that everyone else who auditioned had also been chosen. Some of the older members of the group had cars and provided transport to and from the various venues where we played. One of the people I remember well was Brendan Wade who lived not too far from us in Cabra West, he was a great singer with a beautiful tenor voice. We played in a lot of school halls and parish halls around Dublin. I remember one trip that brought us all the way up country to the village hall in Dunboyne, County Meath.

There was one hospital in particular that we played in where all of the patients were confined to their respective Wards and we were to play on a stage in another part of the complex. There was a large room with a stage, on which there was a microphone that was rigged up to the hospital P.A. system.

The original Belvedere Beats on RTE in 1967. L-R: Jeweller Roe, Noel Preston (drummer), Michael O'Brien, Martin Coffey, Willie Dowling and Robert Gallagher

And there I was standing there about to do my thing when suddenly the two doors of the hall burst open and in ran a woman patient with no clothes on and two nurses running after her, I didn't know what to do, so I just played on. For two years I played in almost every hospital in Dublin and in particular I remember one Christmas time playing in Cappagh Hospital to all the children and nurses.

I well remember one time in particular when my brother Brendan convinced me to pawn my guitar. It was mid-week and he was broke, he hadn't a penny to his name and he wanted to go out that night. So, with me and my guitar on the crossbar of his bike he cycled into Rafter's pawn shop in Gardiner Street. Now, at that time I wasn't too clear on how things worked with pawn shops and so Brendan took the time to explain it all to me and it went something like this, *"You give the man your guitar and he'll give you money for it, it's like a loan. And then when you want your guitar back you just pay him back the money he gave you, and that's all".*

It certainly seemed like a good plan except I wasn't getting the money, Brendan was but we did it anyway. Now, the problem arose on the following Saturday morning when the two of us went back to Rafter's for my guitar. We walked in as casual as you like and Brendan puts the money up on the counter. That was the moment when everything went haywire for me because your man behind the counter says *"Have you got the ticket"?* He told me that he had given me a ticket the other day. *"Oh..."* says I *"...I threw that away, I thought it was just an oul receipt".* And that was that, no ticket no guitar. So, it was back to the Credit Union again.

The Belvedere Beats 2019
Willie Dowling, Noel Preston, Michael O'Brien
and Martin Coffey

These were exciting times for a fourteen to sixteen-year-old who played the guitar most every weekend and who was out there on stage. I never ended up as Elvis or anything like him but I did enjoy it none the less. I think I played in every band that never made it. Except one that is, in 1967 I was a member of the Belvedere Newsboys Club in Marlborough Street. I tried my hand at the boxing for a few weeks and then discovered that a new guitar class was starting up, so I hung up my gloves. This class took me much further than I was in my guitar playing at home.

Then coming up to Christmas time the Belvedere Newsboys Club was approached by RTE television studios and asked if they could provide some entertainment for a special show on youth clubs that was to be aired over Christmas. And that's how I became a member of the first ever Boy Band to appear on Irish television, that was in 1967. In 2019 the surviving members of that little band came together for a reunion night with former members of the Belvo Club and we had a great night, no rehearsals before, just get up in front of the microphone and off we went. So, that's my story of how I became involved in music and the guitar.

Day out in Dollymount

Story Forty-One

Noel Coffey 1963

The Cuckoo Clock

Now, way back in the 1970's, my brother Noel came home on holiday from England. While he was strolling around town one day, he wandered into Hector Grey's shop. It was here that he put his eye on a lovely Cuckoo Clock which he bought. Now, if you keep in mind the political situation going on at that time with England and Ireland and in particular with the troubles in the North, you should get the gist of this story. It was also a time when drugs were beginning to find their way into Ireland and in particular to Dublin.

Now, where the brother lived in England there was a massive British Army Barracks and most soldiers being posted to Belfast at that time went from this barracks. So, the whole town was practically an army base. My brother was kind of young and innocent of a lot of things back then but he was a very good and honest kind of fella. So, when he arrived back home in England and full of excitement at the thought of the Cuckoo Clock, he could barely wait to open it and have it set up on his wall. The clock was battery operated and the Cuckoo sounded so sweet, my brother was whistling no end in harmony with the Cuckoo.

Now, as he delved further into the packaging that came with the clock his beady eyes spotted something that caught his imagination. There was a small sachet in the box and when he opened it up, a white powder poured out. *"Ah..."* says he to himself, *"...what have we got here"*? He was convinced from that very moment that he had uncovered a drug trafficking ring that was smuggling drugs from China into Dublin. And so, being the good citizen that he is, he wrapped up the clock with the Cuckoo inside and the *"Drugs"* and takes them off to his local Cop Shop, the Police Station.

Now, can you imagine the look on the Station Sergeant's face when an Irishman walks into his Station with a ticking clock under his arm? My brother went on to explain that he bought this clock in Ireland, which is ticking away inside its box. The Copper of course jumps to the wrong conclusion and the next thing is, he is on the phone to the Army Bomb Squad. They all arrive in quick time and my poor brother is standing there, surrounded by armed police and Soldiers.

When the Bomb Expert finally gives the all clear, Noel sees this as his chance to tell his story about the drugs in the Cuckoo Clock.

It's then that the little package of white powder is finally taken out of the box and examined. Well, he thought it was quite hilarious when it was discovered that the white powder in the box was there to keep out any dampness and to protect the Cuckoo from not being able to sing. *"Well..."* says Noel to the Coppers and Soldiers, *"...that's a relief"* and picking up the box heads home with a smile on his face at the thought of him being a good citizen, leaving behind a very embarrassed Sergeant to explain it all. So now, the next time you open up a box and find a little package containing white powder inside you might give a thought to my brother and his act of being a good citizen.

The Gough statue which was blown up by the IRA in 1957

Story Forty-Two

The Old Wood Plane

I did a little bit of work on restoring this old Wood Plane that my father used to keep in his shed. It was all rusted and full of oil mixed with sawdust and oul bits of fluff and dirt, not too unlike himself at times. Now, I have to tell you that he loved his oul shed and everything in it. He could walk into that shed in the pitch black of night and without turning on the light he could put his hand on any nail, screw or hammer that he needed. There was a place for everything and everything had its place. If he ever sent me out to the shed for a screwdriver he'd say *"And don't touch anything else because I'll know if you do"*.

Now, originally, some of the tools that my father had he got from his own father, so they were antiques, they'd been around since the war, the First World War. The oul Grandad had served as a motor mechanic with the British Army in WWI and so that's how he got most of his tools.

I always remember one thing in particular that was in the shed. It was the bottom part of my mother's oul kitchen dresser that they brought with them when they moved out of Town, it was blue and white, my father called it *"Legion of Mary"* blue. He used it as a press in the shed and he kept the Shoe Last, that he used for mending our shoes with, in it. It's where he kept all his important stuff and things no one else was allowed to use, such as his Bit and Brace, that's a thing for drilling holes in wood and he even kept a little bottle of Holy Water in there too.

I suppose in some way my father's shed was a bit like Aladdin's Cave to us kids because you'd never know what you were going to find. There was always the match box full of washers or rusty screws and there was always a Sticking Plaster just in case he cut his finger. He had three or four oul Saws that were never of any use because he'd always have to rub Dripping off the frying pan onto them to make them cut. And he had shelves everywhere and all filled with glass jars of things I never knew the names of and a Mustard Tin with metal rivets that he never used but kept them *"Just in case"*. He had oul bicycle chains hanging up next to a spare bicycle wheel that he found in the local Dump. He had loads of heads off hammers that he was going to fix someday. There were all sorts of bits of timber that he planned on using whenever he got around to building a Hen House.

We had a dinner table in our house and the two ends could pull out to make it longer. One time when my mother was in town we pulled out one of the ends and used the table as a stage coach like in the cowboy pictures. My sisters would sit under the table screaming with fright at the gunfire while the older brothers sat on any chairs we had but the chairs were turned backwards and used like a horse. Myself and the brother were sitting on the piece of the table that was pulled out and one of the older brothers stood up on the saddle of his horse and jumped onto the stagecoach and the next thing was, were heard a groan and a crack as the table piece shattered into bits with the weight of us on it.

Now, that's a story in itself. But this turned out to be another job for my father to fix in his shed. I remember going out to watch him working on it. He had a fag in his mouth with a great big long ash and I just wanted to reach up and knock it off but he wasn't in the best of form so I kept my hands down by my side. Eventually my father fixed things up but the piece was a good bit shorter than it originally had been and some of us had to scrunch up closer together when we'd be having our dinner.

He even had his oul Norton motorbike in the shed but it was broken, he was going to fix that someday as well and then there was the great big bucket pram that my mother used to send the brothers to the Park with to collect the turf that nobody wanted, or so she told us. There were also rubber tubes out of bicycle wheels that were punctured but never got repaired. He had loads of tins of oul paint that also came from the local Dump and paint brushes that were rock hard. But would we change him? I don't think so, he is the only Da' we ever had and he did his best for us all. And if I could have him back for a day, I don't think I'd clean the rust off him or try to restore him like his oul Wood Plane, I think I'd prefer him just as he is, the Da'.

Tonge and Taggart roadside water pump

Story Forty-Three

Kathleen Dillon and Joni Tormey

Rainy Days

Do you ever remember coming home from school on a wet rainy day and you drenched to the skin? Well there's one time in particular that I remember well when myself and the brother arrived home from Finbarr's School drenched to the skin like two little sponges filled up with water. As we walked along, we could hear the squelching of the rain water in our little wellies and our stockens had slid off our feet wrapping themselves around our frozen toes. And the rain was running down the back of our necks, down through our shirts and on down the back of our little legs. We hadn't an overcoat or a hat to wear for protection from the elements. Our school books and copies were ruined and soggy, not that we really cared about them too much.

When we eventually arrived at our hall door my brother reached up and pushing open the letter box pulled out the piece of string that held the door key. As he pushed in the door he let out a roar *"Ma' we're home"*. The Ma' came running down the hall and started wiping the rain off our faces with her apron. *"Quick, get them clothes off you or you'll catch your death of cold"* she said. With all our wet clothes, wellies, socks, trousers and schoolbags left at the bottom of our stairs we ran in our nude into the kitchen area of our house.

The first thing that hit us was the smell of home-made soda bread that the Ma' had just taken out of the oven. With our tongues hanging out we made straight for the blazing turf fire to try and get some feeling back into all those little places and things that boys have.

Well do you know what it is, the next thing is the Ma' puts two big plates of stew on the table for us. Talk about hunger, bejakers it's great sauce altogether. We were like two little greyhound pups racing after a rabbit across a field as we made a mad dash for the table. While we were gulping down the spuds and dumplings the Ma' put out a plate of her home-made soda bread on the table. Well now that bread was like nothing on earth. It was almost like we had died and gone straight to Heaven without even seeing Saint Peter himself. There wasn't a word said between the brother and myself the whole time we sat at the table.

When we finally finished stuffing ourselves, we were handed two big mugs of hot sweet tea. It really was a meal fit for a king. Now back then we didn't wear pyjamas to bed, to be honest we never heard of such things. What we wore were called Shimmies, they were like a long nightdress for boys, well that's what the Da' said anyway. So on went the Shimmies and back to the fire we went, fed watered and happy. And do you know what, in next to no time the two of us were fast asleep, huddled up together on my granny's old armchair like two little kittens. I can tell you now in all honesty, there's no cooking or baking like the Ma's, sure she'd make a holy show of all those ones cooking and baking on the telly with their little bits of lettuce on a plate, raw meat and a squirt of HP sauce on the side… *'Thank's Ma', you're great"*.

Story Forty-Four

The Da's Shed

As far back as I can recall my father always had some kind of a shed in our back garden. In the early days when our family first moved to Cabra West from town, himself and his pals would go on a scavenger hunt to the local dump in search of materials to build the shed with. Any old piece of timber was sure to come in handy and especially if it was full of old nails and screws because he would have my brothers at it all day long pulling them out and trying to straighten them with an old hammer, that also came from the dump, well the head did anyway because he made the handle for it himself out of a broken sweeping brush handle. My father had a great pair of hands for fixing things to his satisfaction, which wasn't necessarily to my mother's satisfaction. It's like the time when one of the wheels came off of our pram. Now I have to tell you that the Ma' needed that pram because it served as anything from a baby carriage to a shopping trolley and a turf carrier.

On this one day in particular one of my sisters was pushing the pram up along the Old Cabra Road from Manor Street where the Ma' had sent her for a bit of shopping. In the pram there was a four stone bag of potatoes along with three of us kids as well as a whole pile of small bits of wood that we had found down near the Cattle Market. We also had a pillow case full of stale bread from a bakery and three turnips we found by the side of the road.

By the time we reached the old Yellow Dairy near Cabra Cross my sister had just about had enough of us and our moaning. *"I'm cold, I'm hungry, are we nearly there yet"* and so on, it would go. Now I think the old pram as well had had enough because all of a sudden one of the wheels broke off and the pram tilted over to one side and threw us all out on to the path, as well as the bag of spuds and everything else. I was only five years old at that time and was the one picked out to run home and tell my mother what had happened. Well, eventually we all made it home with the help of the older brothers and a few of their pals.

Now, when my father arrived home from work on his bicycle, he was mobbed by us kids who were as keen as mustard to tell him what had happened and how the brothers and their pals all came to our rescue. *"No worries..."* says he*"...I'll fix that in next to no time* *at all"*. So off to his shed he went with a few of us trailing along behind him like the *"Seven Little Dwarfs"*. Now, to us going into my father's shed was like entering *"Aladdin's Cave"*, because it was full *of "Man Things"* that were full of mystery and magic to us and my father was like *"Merlin the Magician.*

Now his one piece of pride and joy in his shed was the bottom part from our old kitchen dresser that once stood in our kitchen painted in *'Legion of Mary'* blue as he used to say. This was his treasure chest where he kept all his tools and bits of old twine and shoe laces in one draw and bent nails and screws of every description in the other. In the bottom part of the press, where my mother used to keep the breadbin, my father kept an old rusty saw and an old crowbar. He was always sure to remind us to keep our hands in our pockets. *"Don't touch anything, I know where everything is, leave it back where you got it from"*. These were warnings that came with the territory and you had to make sure to abide by these rules or you were forever banned from his shed.

So, after a few minutes of head scratching and puffing on his cigarette he would begin the job of repairing the old pram. Out would come his Hand Drill, that's like one of them kitchen contraptions that my mother uses when she's mixing Custard Powder and milk together. Then out comes his Hacksaw with a blade on it that has less teeth than a new born baby. When he had all his bits and pieces assembled together, he'd light up a fag and after a few puffs he'd be as right as rain. *"Right lads..."* he'd say with a great big grin on his face *"...I have it all worked out now""* With the light outside fading fast he'd be off, cutting this and hammering that, while all our little faces looked on in wonderment. And as sure as anything, in next to no time at all there it was, a wonder to behold, our pram was fixed. Well the axle at least was fixed.

Out comes my mother to have a look at his handiwork. She put a few of us little ones in the pram and as she was wheeling it up and down the yard, another one of the wheels came off. And stating the obvious of course she says *"That won't do at all, sure there's another wheel off"*. My father takes one of them great big deep breaths that only Da's can take. *"Well you see..."* he says *"...I'll have to go up to the dump on Saturday to see if I can find a piece to fit on that and then I'll fix it proper when I get the time. Meanwhile, just take it easy until then"*.

Well the thing is, he never did seem to get the time to go back to that oul pram of ours because it was still like that three years later. There we'd be running home from the turf depot with the pram full to the brim with sacks of turf and all of a sudden off would come the wheel and off would come the turf. And that's how it was in our Da's shed all them years ago.

Story Forty-Five

The Picture House

On this particular day I called in to see my oul pal, Ambrose O'Shea, about some business. Later, on leaving his house I drove up onto Fassaugh Avenue and turning right headed in towards town. I almost always drive slowly along this section of Cabra West, passing by the two sets of shops and the big church on my way. I would sometimes stop my car and open the doors to let my memory out one side and my imagination out the other and watch them both run wild with excitement. Sometimes I might even park my car by the shops and go for a stroll, listening to the accents and the craic that is so much a part of the area. As I drove my car down the hill passing the old Playground on my right and the place where the old Turf Depot once stood on my left, I decided to drive around onto Quarry Road and say hello to the Cabra Grand Picture House. Now, there's a place full of memories.

I passed by the statue of Holy Mary standing in the middle of the road where Quarry Road, Fassaugh Avenue and Fassaugh Road all meet. I always give her a little nod hello and sometimes she'll give me a wink of acknowledgement or maybe just a little smile that says *"I remember you and your gang"*. Sometimes I might even stop off and have a chat with her. I remember one time I asked her did she not get cold standing out there all day. *"Ah no..."* she said *"...sure I have me cloak on over me shoulders. That keeps the breeze off me back"*. *"Well..."* said I *"...do you want a cup of tea or anything"*? *"Ah no, your alright love..."* said she. *"...but thanks anyway"*.

She told me another time that she was glad the number 12 bus wasn't running anymore. *"Now the fumes from that bus used to kill me chest, you know what I mean..."* This remark was followed by a little cough. *"...and the state of me hair from all the chimbly smoke..."* Holy Mary always sounded a bit like the Ma' and as a young boy I'd often wonder did they both go to the same school together because the Ma's name was Mary as well and she went to Rutland Street School.

I drove around by the old Dispensary where all the school children from years ago were brought to get their Polio Sugar Lump. They were all herded along the road like cattle going to the market in Prussia Street with their schoolteachers keeping them all in line. I slowed down as I passed by the houses on my right, what we called *"The Soldiers Houses"*. To me as a young boy growing up in Cabra West these houses always looked big and strong with two pillars of Wicklow granite that look like soldiers guarding the entrance to the houses. It was here that I decided to park my car.

The day was clear and dry but still had a slight chill in the air. With my camera shoved not too deeply into my pocket I decided to walk up by the side of the old Picture House to see if I could get some good photographs of the original building. Sure enough, there it stood, still standing tall and proud as ever, perhaps even looking a little worse for wear at sixty-five years of age. *"Sure, who isn't"* says you. The great thing about this building is that it is still in use today as much as it originally was, or perhaps a bit more so because of the Bingo starting off at one o' clock in the day and still going strong until late into the night when all the Bingo players have to go home to their beds. *"On its own, number one, Kelly's Eye"*.

While I was clicking away with my camera, I could still hear the gangs of young boys and girls chatting away and shouting with excitement as they queued up on a Sunday afternoon along this side of the Picture House and they all bursting at the seams to get inside to lay claim to their favourite seats. I could see all the little pals holding onto each other as tightly as they could so as not to get separated as the side doors opened and they all pushing forward to be first into the building. *"Here, let her pass, she's me pal and we always sit together".* Then of course we had to come face to face with the villain of the peace. And there he stood, the great big tall usher in his red showband style uniform with a stripe down each leg of his trousers and a bus conductor's cap sitting on his head. He'd be hopping from one foot to the other threatening everyone with his great big torch as if he was John Wayne or someone. *"Don't be pushing and shoving, take your time or else",* he'd shout out. *"Here, were you barred last week"* he would ask some young fella. With a terrified look on his face the boy quickly answered, *"Eh, no Mister, that was me brother".* That's how you played it safe back then, you always gave your brother's name or your pal's name when you were in trouble.

After a while of clicking on my camera and reminiscing I strolled back down the laneway and walked towards the main entrance into the cinema. Straightaway I could picture in my mind's eye all of the young couples lined up outside on a Sunday night. The lads with their moths and the moths with their fellas. All as proud as Punch with the girl linking her man and he smoking away on a cigarette thinking he looked like Kirk Douglas. *"Do you like me Beehive"* she'd ask him. *"Your what"*? he would answer. *"Ah for God's sake, did you not notice I got me hair done for tonight. I went to your one up over the shops, you know your one with the bad breath I told you about"*? Her voice would fade off into the night as the fella's mind focused on how well his hair looked with all the

Brylcream he'd put in it earlier, kind of like Elvis in a way or maybe James Dean, *"The Rebel Without A Cause"*.

The original front of the cinema is still in place as are the two buildings on both sides. To the right of the main entrance there was always a Chip Shop on the ground floor. If a couple had any money left over after buying popcorn and ice cream, they would often buy a bag of chips with plenty of salt and vinegar splashed over them to eat on their way home. On the left side of the building there was a Sweet Shop and up overhead was a surgery run by Doctor Sammy Davis. These offices and shops were all part of the original cinema building.

The cinema was officially opened on the 17th of April in 1949 and had seating for 1,600 people and included an upstairs balcony area. I remember coming across something in the papers a few years back about an incident in the Cabra Grand. Some young fella from Quarry Road got into trouble for hitting one of the ushers and ended up in court over it. He got a one-year prison sentence and was also fined £1 for tearing the usher's tunic.

In the early days you could sit and watch a talent show or see some form of live entertainment on the stage before the house lights would dim and the curtain begin to rise. On some Sunday afternoons a man called Billy Panama would appear on stage demonstrating his skills with a YoYo, *"Walk the Dog"* or *"Rock the Cradle"* were some of his favourites. As the curtain began rising a great big sea shell would appear to open up on the screen behind it.

A loud roar of excitement would rise up from all of the young children seated in the auditorium below.

Sometimes the guitar music of The Shadows or Duane Eddie would play out over the speaker system allowing people time to find and settle into their seats. Years ago, you certainly got your monies worth when you went to the Pictures. They would show or a short cartoon, followed by the Path News that always showed the Queen of England going around the world and sometimes they'd show *"Gideon of Scotland Yard"*, which was all about murder in London.

Then you could have a Trailer, short clips of what films were due to be shown in the cinema the following week. On other occasions you would see what we called *'The Follow N' Upper'*. This was an adventure film which was shown over a period of several weeks with fifteen to twenty-minute segments shown each week. Each scene would end with a dramatic clip which left punters sitting on the edge of their seats trying to guess what was about to happen next. A small film would then be shown followed by the 'Big Picture' and hopefully for the boys it was a cowboy film. If it was a haunty (Horror) film the girls would all duck under their coats or cardigans and start screaming with pretended fright.

And of course, you always had an Interval, that's when the curtain would roll down like waves on the sea and the house lights would come on again. A gang of young boys and girls would make a mad dash for the toilets, girls to the left and boys to the right. From the back of the cinema one of the usherettes would walk down the aisle with a large tray filled with small tubs of ice cream, ice pops, chocolates and other goodies. The tray had a strap that went across the girl's shoulders and around her back. If you were cute enough you could slip your hand in under her elbow from behind and snatch something off the tray.

On the odd occasion myself and my pals would crawl on the floor underneath our seats looking for any bits of chewing gum that people had spat out or thrown away. We'd get an extra chew from it before we too would spit it out or stick it into the hair of a girl sitting in front of us. Sometimes you might be lucky enough to find a sweet still in its wrapper or one stuck to the floor. Other times we'd go looking for a disused ice cream carton and clean it out with our fingers. Then we'd run off to the toilet with it and use it as a cup for collecting water in to drink. One of us would flush the toilet chain while the other held the cup inside the toilet bowl and caught the water as it flushed down from the overhead cistern. Is it any wonder that we turned out the way we did?

As I walked up the couple of marble steps at the entrance to the Picture House and in through the main doors I could still feel that sense of excitement that I experienced all those years ago. I thought back to the time when I first went to the pictures in this cinema at night. I was only thirteen years old and therefore would have been considered too young by the usher for admittance. If the usher noticed you going in for an evening show he would make sure not to allow you in to an early show with the young children. He'd make sure you paid for an adult ticket.

*The Third Amendment of the Constitution Act 1972 is
an amendment to the Constitution of Ireland that permitted
the State to join the European Communities, which would later
become the European Union, and provided that European
Community law would take precedence over the constitution*

Anyway, on this particular occasion my older brother had decided to go to the evening film and asked me to go with him. At first, I refused because of my young age. Then my father got a bright idea and dressing me up in his overcoat and cap and shoving my feet into a pair of his old wellies, sent me off with my brother. I was told to keep my head down and not to look at the usher as we walked in and it worked. But I must have looked a right sight strolling down Killala Road with my brother while my father and mother stood at their hall door waving us off. *'The innocence of youth'* says you. If you look on the floor inside the main door you can still see the name of the cinema emblazoned in mosaic styled tiles. *'Cabra Grand Cinema'* is what it still proudly announces.

I suppose the first thing that struck me as I entered the building was the absence of smell, the strong, almost aromatic smell of freshly made popcorn that greeted everyone all those years ago as they made their way up to the ticket window. *'Two tickets please, up on the balcony and at the back if you can manage it'*, money went one way and tickets went the other. My Da' used to tell us not to bring the girlfriend to a good film that we wanted to see because we'd miss most of it with all the snogging that would go on. Do you now, back then my Da' knew about a lot of things that we didn't know. When you handed your tickets to the usher, he'd tear them in two and hand you back one half. The other half was stabbed through the heart with a Sack Needle that had a long piece of twine on the other end. And there straight in front of you was the lady working the popcorn machine. Next to the actual pictures this was the main attraction for us youngsters. The Popcorn Lady always wore a white shop coat and had red lipstick on as well. There was a little pot that she put the popcorn kernels into and then all of a sudden, they'd all start to pop and burst out from under the lid of the pot. This was almost better entertainment than we'd see on the stage inside.

On your left as you entered the foyer was the sweet counter but as children, we never bought any sweets from there because they were in bags and cost too much money. We'd stuff out pockets full of sweets that we'd bought in the Sweet Shop next door. The manager's office was also on the left as you walked in. I never knew the names of any of the managers that worked there over the years. Directly across the foyer area were the stairs leading up to the balcony. The price for a balcony seat was dearer than the price of a seat downstairs. If you arrived late or walked in as the picture was about to start everything would appear pitch black until your eyes became accustomed to the dark. Then almost immediately the usher or usherette would blind you by shining their torch in your face.

I was somewhat taken aback when I walked through the doors into the auditorium and saw the place fitted out as a Bingo Hall. I was half expecting to see all of the original cinema seats still in place and I especially wanted to see the double seats that they used to have dotted around where young courting couples could sit even closer together. *"Take your hand off me knee, here's your Woodbine back"*. Now me and my pals usually sat in the seats over on the left-hand side or should I say that's where the usher dictated, we sat there so he could keep an eye on us. Now if you happened to strike it lucky and got off with a moth the pair of you would then move over to the seats on the far side of the cinema, as far away from the gang as possible.

As I stood looking around the Bingo Hall, I could still pick out some of the original fittings that were familiar to me as a young boy. The boys' toilets were still on the right side and the girls' toilet over on the left and most of the old wall fittings were still in place. It certainly had that feeling of familiarity about it. Now, if you could take away all of the bingo stuff and put back in place all of the old cinema seats then almost everything would be returned to its original condition.

I walked up onto the stage and looking back into the auditorium my heart sank as I noticed that the balcony area was all boarded off as it is no longer in use. While standing there looking out over all the seats I wanted to shout out the names of the boys and girls I knew from all those years ago. *"Would the following boys and girls please stand up because you're all going to get a free bag of popcorn. Tony Norton, Georgie McCluskey, Phyllis Wyatt, Liam Kelly, Anne Reddin, Wang Fagan, Pat McCabe, Noel Murray, Colm Russell, Ambrose and Noelie O'Shea, Willier Kavanagh, Andy Lyons, Carmel Bell, Marie Kelly, Tango Flood and PJ Kavanagh. The rest of you all have to pay for your own"*.

Eventually I had to whisper a fond goodbye to all my pals and let them get on with watching the film, it was *"Whistle Down the Wind"* with Hayley Mills. She was my first love, you know. I fell head over heels in love with her in 1962 as I watched that film right there in the Cabra Grand. I remember myself and my pal hiding in the boys' toilets so that we could watch it a second time. So, with all my memories safely tucked under my arm and my poor camera worn out from all the photographs I'd taken, I headed out. *"Ladies and Gentlemen, the King is leaving the building..."*

Cabra Boys Scouts on parade

Story Forty-Six

The Catechism

I used to love my Catechism when I was a young fella, I always felt real holy when I'd have it in my hands. *"Who made the world"*, I used to love it when the Nun would ask us that question because I knew the answer off by heart. There were so many questions and answers we had to learn for our First Holy Communion. And I remember the Nun giving us a little bit of an ice cream wafer and telling us to pretend it was Holy Communion. I got a clatter off her because I asked her did it have some of Jesus blood in it. There were two classes of boys making their First Holy Communion and we had to go into their classroom and stand around the wall because there was no room at any of the desks for us to sit down.

My little legs used to be killing me from all the standing because one of them was broken when I was knocked down by a car at four years of age. We used to get crayons and colour in the pictures in the Catechism and I remember my pal who was sitting beside me in the desk giving Baby Jesus red hair.

I always remember when my father used to bring home brown paper from work and we'd spend the whole time after our tea covering our school books with it. And because there were so many of us kids in the family some of us had wallpaper to cover our books with. We'd have to borrow my mother's good scissors from her sewing box to cut the paper with and she'd always get my father to sharpen it with a file from out of his shed when we were finished.

We used to use wet soap to stick the paper on the books, we didn't have any glue but my father had a small bottle of Gum that he used for sticking postage stamps with, the stamps that arrived on Christmas Cards that hadn't a Post Office mark on them. We used to put any left-over brown paper on our school copies as well. You'd be real chuffed the next day in school and you taking out your school book with the brand-new brown paper on it. I used to draw an Angel on the brown paper on the front of my Catechism and it would take me ages because I wanted it to look special for God.

And I remember the Nun told us one time that if we were good Catholics there would always be a Priest nearby if we were knocked down by a bus and we were dying. So, after that, if I ever saw a Priest while I was out and about, I'd never cross the road in case I was hit by a bus. Now I have to tell you that there was no Priest around when I was knocked down at four years of age but maybe that's because my brother Noel was bringing me with him and his gang to rob an orchard.

I couldn't wait to make my First Holy Communion because I knew once I did that I'd go straight to Heaven if I died. Every night I used to lie in my bed, next to my two brothers, praying to Holy God to let me see what Heaven was like, I nearly went religious mad at that young age.

I remember one time our Teacher told us to write a story about what we thought Heaven would be like. My imagination went off like a rocket going into space, I couldn't write fast enough. I could see all the Holy Angels with clean faces dancing in a circle around Holy Mary and throwing bunches of flowers at her feet and she smiling back at them with delight.

And I could see a great big table with bowls of ice cream on it and bags of marshmallows with hot custard poured over them. There was loads of Christmas puddings hanging up in holy pillow cases and Holy God was eating bread and jam with his cup of tea. Eventually the Teacher had to take the pencil out of my hand to stop me writing anymore.

Story Forty-Seven

The Television Seat

Why this became known as *"The Television Seat"* I don't know. In the early 1960's that's what some of the Bus Conductor's used to call it. I remember one time, when I was about fifteen years old, while I was on my way home from work, I had to sit in the seat facing this long seat. And it just happened to be my good misfortune that a drunk sat on the long seat facing me.

And you know how it is in situations like this. I was drenched to the skin from the rain that pelted down while I stood with a mob, no orderly queues back then, waiting on the bus. And I can tell you, I was in no form for talking to anyone, I just wanted to get home, have my dinner and go out to my pals. The bus was filled to capacity, standing room only and upstairs for smoking. Along came the Conductor, rattling some change in his hand and roaring out *"Fares please now, ladies and gentlemen"*. I handed him my fare and put the ticket in my pocket. Then he looked at the drunk and repeated his request for fares. Your man looked up at the Conductor and started singing at the top of his voice, *"There's a hole in the bucket dear Liza, dear Liza..."* The whole bus went into an uproar, I even think the bus driver was having a good laugh as well as the people upstairs. The stern-faced Conductor wasn't amused, he looked at the drunk and said *"If you want to sing on this bus you'll have to get off at the next stop"*. Money quickly changed hands with a mouthful of muttering coming out of the drunk.

Now, of all things, the drunk looks at me and says, *"Well, what do you think of that, son..."*? My poor brain refused to engage with my tongue. *"...there's gratitude for yeah"* he said. Then he looked at the Oul One sitting beside me. She wasn't taking any notice of him either. Then he says *"Here Misses, don't I know you"*? She continued to ignore him. Then he's off again with another song. *"We'll meet again, don't know where, don't know when..."* And it is at this point that my brain shuts down completely.

Eventually the bus arrives at my stop. The drunk is fast asleep with his head resting on the shoulder of the Oul Fella beside him. My brain is still in shut-down until I get off the bus and its then that the rain wakes me up.

Story Forty-Eight

Looking Back

The house seems unusually quiet as I stand looking out of the window from my parent's upstairs bedroom. An old neighbour passes by down below with her head bent against the drizzling rain. She has her shopping bag tucked tightly underneath her arm as she struggles to retain her footing. Her headscarf is tightly knotted under her chin as she squints through eyes that have long ago lost their bright twinkle of youth. Is she the woman that my mother told me about whose husband had left home and went to England in search of work? According to my mother he was working alright, working on a second family. He never came back to his wife and family here. My memory begins to play tricks as I'm transported back in time and I see two of my sisters playing swings on the lamp-post near our house. The rope wraps itself tightly around the lamp as the girls let out squeals of delight.

The girl next door with the patch over one eye of her glasses is playing with a skipping rope. She almost falls to the ground as her toe catches the rope which then twists around her foot. I shout to her to be careful but of course she can't hear me. Her pals play Piggy Beds on the footpath outside our gate. A young boy dashes past her pushing his bicycle hoop with a small stick. As he looks behind, he can see Geronimo and a whole tribe of Indians chasing after him. He almost knocks one of the girls off balance as she skips from one square of the Piggy Bed to the next. She appears to move in slow motion as she grabs hold of the nearby railings to gain her composure.

In the distance I can hear the Coal Man shouting out in rhythm to the clip clop of his horse's hoofs. One of my older brothers runs out with a bucket in his hand to get it filled with just enough coal to light our fire. One of his socks keeps slipping down his leg and he stops after every few steps to pull it back up again. The Ma' hasn't got enough money for a full bag of coal. The few pieces of turf that we have will compliment the coal later on as the evening turns cold. The fire won't be lit until a few minutes before my Da' is due home. A shiver runs down my spine as a squall of rain hits the bedroom window and brings me back to reality.

As I turn away from the window to leave the room, I suddenly see myself, a little boy, sitting in a corner by the fireplace next to my brother, both of us sitting as quiet as little mice. The flames from the burning fire scorch our tiny little spindly legs as we listen to the gentle voice of our mother telling us stories of her childhood days. She is sitting propped up in her bed, gently cradling the latest edition to our family. The rest of her young brood sit gazing into the coloured flames of the fire as it hisses and burns my father's old shoes, shoes that were too tired and worn out to be of any use to him. That's how my father said he felt when he had to retire from his job, tired and worn out.

As I turn again to the bedroom window, I suddenly hear voices raised in song coming along the street. It's a May Procession and it's coming down our road. The local Boy Scouts are leading the parade carrying a Virgin Mary statue. One of the Scouts isn't as tall as the other three and struggles to hold up his side of the statue. The Parish Priest seems oblivious to any distractions around him. He appears to be in a state of religious euphoria. Holy Mary however turns her head about and smiles at the crowds of cheering neighbours. For a very brief moment I was sure that she looked up at our window and gave me a wink.

Slowly the singing voices fade off into the distance and all becomes quiet as before. As I turn away from the bedroom window, I'm confronted by a metal grill in front of my face. I'm suddenly surrounded by darkness and an old familiar smell of burning incense is circulating about my head. It is then that I realise I'm in a

Confession Box. Behind the sliding wooden window, I can hear the Priest breathing and muttering to himself. My nose is pressed up against the metal grill and my little bare knees are sore from kneeling on the wooden floor. I can feel my heart hammering and pounding inside my little chest.

Suddenly the shutter opens with a bang and I'm overcome by the smell of whiskey from the Priest. And all of a sudden and without even thinking, out it comes, *"Bless me Father for I have sinned, well I think I have. It's donkey years since my last confession Father"*. My mind goes into auto pilot as I tell him a load of lies about things I didn't do. I begin to stutter with nerves when the Priest slams the shutter and throws me into total darkness once again. I can't remember what he said to do for my penance but it sounded like *"Where's that bloody bottle gone"*.

I then find myself back in my parent's bedroom. The rain has finally stopped and the time has come for me to leave. I look across the room and see the two little boys waving me goodbye. My mother also smiles up at me from the comfort of her bed. From the toilet across the way I can hear my father singing. He must be shaving because that's the only time he sings in our toilet. That's when the curtain comes down and the lights go off, exit stage left.

Story Forty-Nine

There's No Place Like Home

The house I grew up in in Cabra West was always home to me, no matter where I lived. I always remember my father, writing letters to my older siblings who lived in England, asking them when would they be home, he meant on holiday of course but as a young boy I always thought it was strange that he would still use that term when they no longer lived at home. I didn't understand back then, as I do now, that home is always home no matter where we live. And my siblings who lived in England were the same, always talking about going home. Even today, while some of them have lived abroad for almost sixty years, it's still refered to as home. They too would write letters saying that they were planning a trip over on the boat and looking forward to going home. The Da' would sometimes phone them from the Phone Box around the corner from us and he might only get three minutes for his money but at least, for those in England, it was a call from home.

Sometimes a knock would come at our hall door and some fella or young one from our road would be there, home on holiday from living in England and dropping in to see the Ma' and Da'. Sometimes they'd be brought into the parlour and served up cups of tea while they chatted away about their new lives in England. They would tell of the excitement of getting on the boat for the first time and how rough the crossing was and then sitting on the train for hours as it whizzed through the dark English countryside. They would talk about all of the people on the boat and little children crying all the way over and of course there was always a story about some drunk or other getting sick all over the place. Of course, the Ma' and Da' had heard similar stories hundreds of times before but they always made sure to let their visitor feel it was the first time to hear their story.

And sometimes they'd even bring a little present for the Ma', you know, one of them little ornaments with a sticker on them from Liverpool or Manchester. It would always be put in our China Cabinet so it wouldn't get broken, we had loads of them little things and each one had a story attached to it about who brought it and where they were living in England and how they were getting on. I remember in recent years when the Ma' took one out and showed it to me and then told me of the story behind it. How, soon after arriving in Birmingham, he took to the drink and couldn't hold down a job and the babies came, one on top of the other and the poor wife, too ashamed of course to let her family back home know the truth of her situation. She was best pals with my older sister when they were in school together and the Ma' remembered when she got married and the great wedding they had with the sit-down dinner in her own mother's house with cabbage, potatoes and cornbeef served up to all the guests. She remembered how happy this young couple looked with stars in their eyes and love in their hearts.

Mister Bradley brought them out to the boat in his lorry and the whole road of women and girls crying their eyes out at their going. That's how the Ma' told it to me and I could see she was a little upset as to how that young girl's life had spanned out. No happy ending there I'm afraid.

When my own siblings came home on holiday they would always stay in our house, they'd sleep on the bedsetee in our parlour and their cases would be in there as well. Our house would be well and truely polished a week before their arrival and we'd be warned to be on our best behaviour or else. We always got our breakfast first, a cup of tea and a slice of bread and margarine and then out we'd be sent. The older adults all sat down to a fry for their breakfast, when they'd arrive in from the boat they were always sat down at our table and served the same breakfast. They loved it of course, real Irish sausages, black pudding and rashers, fried bread and a cup of Lyons Tea. The sister often said that there was nothing like a real Irish breakfast. The lodging house that she stayed in only gave her toast and marmalade with her cup of tea for breakfast. I always wanted to tell her that all we ever got was a lump of porridge and a cup of tea before we were sent off to school.

When their own kids got a bit older they'd be put in bed beside us to sleep, we didn't mind of course because they always had loads of sweets and we made them share them out with us. My brother used to be teaching them how to curse and say bad words. I remember one time seeing my older brother arriving off the boat in Dunlaoghaire and shaking my Da's hand and saying *"It's great to be home Da"*. In recent times he told me of how strange it was for him coming home because he was a visitor now, home on holiday, things had changed, the younger ones in the family were all grown up now, he was home but he felt like he really didn't fit in as he once did. That's also how I felt when I came home from living in England. Even my oul pals had changed, they were all too busy mottin' and some of them were even married.

And then the day comes when the home, the nest, is no longer there, the Da' is not in Dunlaoghaire to meet you coming off the boat, the Ma' is not frying up a breakfast for you anymore. They have passed on and the house has been sold, strangers live there now. But I still call our house, number 36, home, and I haven't lived there in 50 years. I suppose it's all of the happy memories I carry with me that pulls me back to it. There were some sad ones of course but in general, my memories of home are thankfully, very happy.

Story Fifty

His last words

I had decided that if I wanted a few private moments with my father I would either have to go to the hospital late at night or very early in the morning. Early in the morning suited me best. My father was lying in the hospital dying of cancer and wasn't aware of it. He knew of course that he was unwell but not to the extent that his family knew. He was placed on his own in a small room off the main corridor. There wasn't much room for visitors with the machines he was hooked up to. I was quite aware that this was probably the last and final time I would ever see him alive. My mind was filled with confused messages. Yes, I wanted him out of pain and no, I didn't want him to die. It was a catch twenty-two situation with too many catches.

I stood outside in the hospital corridor for a few minutes looking at him through the blinds on the window of his room, probably trying to blind myself to the reality of his situation. A young nurse was trying her best to make him as comfortable as she could. He looked so weak and helpless. That was how I felt, weak and helpless, unable to help my father at a time when I felt he needed me most. I thought then of the time when he brought me to the Children's Hospital and the doctor wanted to give me an injection. I was probably about three years old. He held me in his arms and told me to squeeze him tightly. He said that I could squeeze all of the pain into him, that he wouldn't feel a thing because he was a big man. I never felt a thing. It was at that very moment I wished he could squeeze me and release all of his pain into me. I just felt so sad and so helpless.

He was very pale and weak, hardly able to raise his head off the several pillows that afforded him some support. *"Martin I'm not well,"* he said in a faint and whispering voice. These were to be the last words he would ever speak to me. I took my comb out of my back pocket and combed his grey hair neatly across his head. I then gently held his hand in mine and placed my other hand on his head, ever so quietly stroking his grey hair. He looked up at me with his heavenly blue eyes wanting to speak but unable to find the strength to utter a single word. I spoke for him instead. I told back to him some of the stories of his childhood that he had shared with me over the years, naming his schoolboy pals and his Aunt May who reared him after his mother died, reminding him of all that he did for us, his fifteen kids and of his love for my mother.

Beside his bed he had two pictures that I had given him on an earlier visit. Both pictures were of old Dublin, scenes of which he was very familiar. Admiral Nelson on his pillar overlooking Dublin and a scene of the Customs House with sail boats tied up on the Liffey. Dublin in the rare old times. I released my hand from his grip and reached over to lift up the pictures. It was then that I realised that instead of me holding his hand he was in fact maintaining a weak grip on mine. I spoke softly to him about the pictures and his memories of times gone by. He had told me these stories over and over again, probably afraid that I'd miss or forget some small important detail of his life. It always felt to me as if every small detail was a link in a chain of events. If one link was missing then the picture as a whole was incomplete.

I asked him if he could remember the last time his mother held him in her arms. His head moved delicately to tell me no. He had long lost the memory of his mother's sweet embrace. I spoke to him of the relationship he enjoyed with his own father. I mentioned the story of his father being arrested in 1913 for riotous behaviour during the Great Lockout with the union leader James Larkin. He managed to force a little smile out of the side of his mouth in response to that story. His father it seems was a bit of a rogue, and probably a big bit at that. I ever so gently held his hand in my two hands and told him of my love for him.

I could feel and taste my own salty tears running down my cheeks as I spoke. There were tears of joy for him and tears of sadness for me. Sometimes the tears would mingle into tears of joy and sadness all at the one time. And so, the conversation went until stillness fell over the room. There was almost a feeling of other unseen people in our presence. It was like when you walk into a darkened cinema and the usherette is standing there waiting to take you to the seat you've been allocated to. At first you don't really see her but gradually she comes into focus, as does the rest of the audience and the auditorium. Your eyes are trying to become accustomed to the lack of light. My father's eyes would have to become accustomed to a different kind of light.

I soon realised that my time had finally come to bid my father a fond farewell. I had to walk away and let him go. Slowly and reluctantly I released his grip from my hands. His blue eyes closing asleep, I stood there crying like a little boy lost, looking down at my frail old dad. In the eyes of a little boy my father always seemed a giant. He could do anything; fix anything, like the broken leaf on our dining table. I watched him in our shed at home measuring and cutting a piece of timber until it took on the required shape of the broken piece. It was probably us kids that broke it in the first place. When he was laid out at home, I slipped a little note into his coat pocket telling him how much I loved him and was going to miss him so. And that's how it was for me when I last spoke to my Da'.

Story Fifty-One

The Reform School

When my grandmother was five years old, she lived with her parents in Dublin. At this time her mother was arrested and brought to court for her part in a murder, later reduced to manslaughter. She was sent to prison for five years. My granny, however, was sent to a Girl's Reform School in Tipperary and remained there until her sixteenth birthday, she served eleven years of a sentence.

Her mother eventually made contact with the school and kept up a correspondence with my granny through the Head Nun. In 1916, my granny received word that her mother, who was now out of prison, was dying and asking to see her. So, granny packed up her life in Tipperary and made her way to Dublin, she hadn't seen her mother in almost seventeen years. Within the space of a couple of months my granny buried her mother, this is her story.

I was only five years old you know
When they took me Ma' away
A policeman came and told me
With the Nun's I'd have to stay
Me Ma' went into prison
To make up for her sins
And I went to the country
To a place I'd never bin

I could see the Rock of Cashel
From my bedroom every morn
So far away, I'd have to stay away
From the place where I was born
The Nun's they all looked after me
From morning until night

They showed me how to sew and knit

And taught me wrong from right

We went to Mass each morning

Where Holy God was looking down

From on the cross where he was hanging

And on his face he had a frown

The Nun's said that me mammy

Put them thorns upon His head

From all the bad things that she did

And the kind of life she led

I told Him I was sorry

For all the things me Ma' had done

I felt so sad and lonely

And I told that to the Nun

She slapped my face

'You're a disgrace

Since the day that you were born'

She said to me

But I couldn't see

That I'd done any wrong

So every day I went to school

With my fondest little pal

She said she was an orphan girl

From a place called Donegal

We learned to read

We learned to write

To add up one and one

And so my days were spent like this

Because of things me Ma' had done

When I was sixteen years of age

The Nun's they put me out

To find my own way in the world

To put food in my mouth

I went to work for Misses Ryan

In a place called Bansha Town

She had a pub, a shop, a farm

And soon I settled down

Misses Ryan was good to me

She loved me as her own

I cleaned and cooked and polished hard

The way the Nun's had shown

I had a letter from me Ma'
From her prison cell it came
It said she missed me ever so
And I was not to blame

For things she'd done and the life she'd led
And the way things were for me
She promised that the day would come
When together we would be.
The years passed by as I grew up
The Ma' she kept in touch
Her prison life was very hard
She hadn't very much

Then they let her out one day
The Ma' they'd set her free
I smiled a smile upon my face
For what was going to be
Then the news it came one day
In a letter from Dublin Town
It said my mother's health was bad
She was rapidly going down

She called for me from her dying bed

She longed to see my face

I longed to sit and hold her hand

And feel her warm embrace

I packed my bags and made my way

To Dublin Town by train

I said farewell to Misses Ryan

Whom I'd never see again

I left old Tipperary Town

My childhood and my youth

As my mother's frail voice called to me

I had to face the truth

She looked so small and frail and weak

As she lay upon her bed

"Ma" I whispered in her ear

As I gently stroked her head

Her eyes they slowly opened

"Annie" she tried to say

As she placed her hand upon my hand

And gently slipped away

◆ ◆ ◆

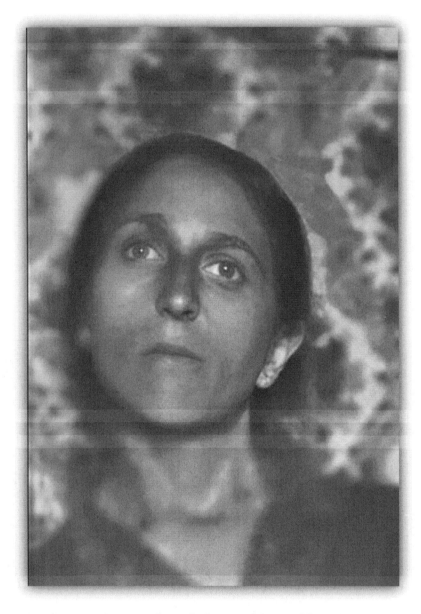

May Doyle reared my father and four of his siblings

*In certain parts of Dublin City, it was not unusual for young
children to be abandoned by their parents*

Story Fifty-Two

Mrs Foran

Ah poor Misses Foran once lived in this room

Way up on Summerhill

She was a great oul crater with a marvellous voice

I can still hear her singing shrill

She had twenty-three children all born in this room

There was Padser and Bridie and Ned
And after that she could never keep
The rest of their names in her head

Her husband was Michael a decent oul skin
Who worked when the weather was good
But spent most of his time in Costello's pub
Codging a drink when he could
He was born in the Monto in Elliott Place
Right next door to a brothel or two
He helped out the Girls by cleaning their rooms
And getting to know who was who

Now poor Misses Foran had a heart of gold
And shared everything she had
With neighbours and strangers and anyone else
In others she never saw bad
And each of her children she sent off to school
She wanted them edumucated
Because she couldn't read and nor could himself
And their lives she didn't want wasted
So here in this room in a tenement house
Misses Foran lived in content

Her kids all grown up the husband he died

And her final years all near but spent

Then Holy God He gave her a call

I need you up here He said

So she laid her head down where her children were born

In that creaky old brass and iron bed

She said a Hail Mary in low whispered tones

Closing her eyes with a sigh

Four Angels stood by from Heaven above

To guide Misses Foran un-high

♦ ♦ ♦

Story Fifty-Three

Sometimes

Sometimes it's just those little things
That brings us to a place
We haven't seen or heard about
An old familiar face

A statue with a broken head
That fell down to the floor
The night my father came home drunk
And fell in through the door

Singing to my mother
While down on bended knee
She laughed out loud
And held his hand
The way they used to be

He knocked the Kitchen Dresser
While lighting up a smoke
The statue took a tumble
And on the floor it broke

They laughed together loud and free
A moment without care
The Holy Man without a head
Lay on the floorboards there

This little broken statue
I found in Da's old shed
I'll leave it for a while he thought
I'll have to glue his head

Like bent old nails and rusty screws
With intentions of the best
The poor old Saint was never fixed
He just joined all the rest

Sometimes it's just those little things
That remind me of my Da'
The love he showed to each of us
And his best pal
My oul Ma'

Story Fifty-Four

The Royal Canal and Broombridge

I took a walk up along the canal and had a great chat with
meself, have a listen…
We talked endlessly about all the pals we remembered from
over the years
the teachers we had in school
what we got for our dinner
what we drank as kids
the games we played

the neighbours we had

the dogs we had

kissing the dead

the kind of house we lived in

all our brothers and sisters

the second-hand shoes we wore

the hand-me-down clothes we wore

people who died

the neighbours out fighting

the Da' fixing a bicycle puncture in the kitchen

the Ma' hanging out the washing

the clubs we joined

our days spent up in the Phoenix Park

robbing orchards

telling lies in Confession

women hanging over the railings having a chat

picking blackberries

help the halloween party

what did you get for Christmas

bent nails and rusty screws

two dogs stuck together

the fifteen acres

funerals on our road

the ragman

the slop man

new babies

people going to England to work

the milkman

the priests in our parish

the holy nun's in school

making ice slides in winter

collecting turf

the May Processions

the Corpus Christi parade

schoolbags

mitching

kittens in a sack

dead dogs

the sister's dolls and pram

smoking behind the Da's shed

collecting jam jars and old newspapers

swimming in the canal

throwing stones at the trains

bonfires

how many easter eggs did you get

the stew-house

bicycles with no tyres

me granny

scutting on lorries

playing nick nack on doors

where babies came from

girls playing skipping and piggy beds

the sisters playing shop with the broken chainie

film stars

my pal who broke his leg in the playground

venetian blinds

net curtains

coats on the bed

christmas pudding hanging up in a pillow case

washing clothes in the bath

the pawn shop

Holy Communion

going to Mass

hoppers in the bed

making toast at the fire

wearing stockings in bed

a plate of coddle

a bowl of stew

cloth nappies boiling on the gas stove

baby's soothers

syrup of figs

the young one with the patch on one side of her glasses

our birthday

the Sunshine House in Balbriggan

a day in Dollymount

dodging our bus fare

chasing girls

playing cowboys and Indians

playing football on the road with a burst ball

kick the can

hoola hoops

making our own swords for a fight

making a snowman

pushing each other on a trolley with real ball bearing
wheels

going to see someone laid out dead

getting slapped in school

Sodality

getting knocked down by a car

going into Woolworth's

santy clause

the playground

playing conkers

First Holy Communion

a bile on our neck

getting washed in the kitchen sink

getting a chase

red rover red rover

fights with other kids

bread and jam

piggy beds

going out to Bray on the train

stingers in a field

silver paper for the black babies

the moving crib

*The father's that went away to England and never came
home again*

The barber who used to spit on our neck

my sister's boyfriend

the Blind Man's shop

the Deaf and Dumb school

sucking on each other's sweets

wearing the brother's shirt to my first dance

going out with a girl

queueing up for the Picture House

my first drink

thinking the Da' new nothing about girls

swapping Comics

doing our ecker

swimming in the canal

the Cabra Baths

looking for money down a shore

killings rats in the Dump

holding a girl's hand

the first kiss

cutting my own hair

the type of music we loved

looking up at the stars

the Da' on his bike

going for long walks

getting a bottle of Lucozade

pals in Artane School

my first guitar

the Gas Man

going to my cousins in town

my uncle away at sea

the Coal Man

drawing on the path with chalk

finding money on the road

Boland's cream buns

The Cattle Market on Wednesday

The Russian Sputnik

Seeing JFK in the Park

Now these are just a few of the things that go through my

head when I go for a walk by my own self.

Story Fifty-Five

School Days Over

It seems like only yesterday

With me schoolbag on me back

I wandered in to this cloakroom

And hung me coat up on the rack

I was only four years old you see

And I didn't want to go

But me Ma' she didn't listen

And me brother told me so

He said to me the school was great

And I'd have lots of fun

I'd get a sambo and some milk

From the Holy Nun

I loved those times when I was here

With my little pals and all

The sun was always shining

As best as I recall

And now I'm back to look around

And see what used to be

My pals are all grown up and gone

And now there's only me

Story Fifty-Six

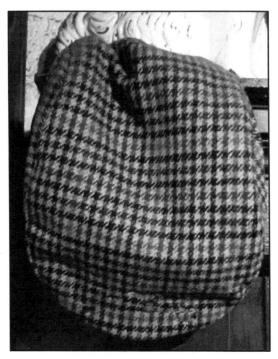

A Monto Tale

Come in says she I know your knock

Hang your cap up on the door

For one and thruppence I'm yours for the night

Sit down and I'll tell yeah more

Pour yourself a glass of stout

Before we lay down on the bed

I'll sing sweet songs of Nightingales

To ease your aching head

Ah Maggie love says he to me
In a smooth and kindly manner
The works been scarce and I'm sorry to say
That I've only got a Tanner

Ah here says I now Mister Doyle
You know I don't come cheap
I've me rent to pay the kids to feed
And me Ma' I have to keep

Says he to me but it's just this once
And I'll square up this day week
There's a ship due in and I'm sure of work
And things won't be so bleak

Come on says I Then just this once
And I don't want any uppence
The next time that you call around
Make sure you've one and thruppence

One and Thruppence

A Tanner

Story Fifty-Seven

(Photograph by Paddy Coffey 1905-1989)

The Rent Man

My mother told me of a practise, that she knew of, by some of the men who collected rents in and around the tenement houses in 1930's Dublin. Now, she stressed it wasn't all of the men who collected the rents that did this, only some of them. Many of these men were ex members of the R.I.C police force. If a poor mother couldn't come up with her rent, and especially if she fell into arrears for several weeks, she could find herself in a position, whereby the

Rent Man, could make certain unsavoury demands on her or one of her children. Faced with this threat, many of the mothers would take to the *"Streets"* to earn enough money to pay off the rent arrears.

The Rent Man called the other day
The woman near got weak
She said she hadn't got a bob
That times are just too bleak
The Rent Man said "It's a month you owe
The money must be found
Otherwise you'll have to send
That young girl there around"

The woman stood in terror
Of what he had to say
She heard it from a neighbour
That he liked to have his way
With young girls like her daughter
Whose innocence he'd destroyed
Her heart it groaned at the very thought
She just sat there and cried

There had to be some other way
For her to pay the rent
So late that night when all was quiet
Out on the street she went

And so, she got the money
Now what else could she do
To keep the wolf at bay once more
To pay off what was due?

But that's the way it was back then
And regardless of the price
When the Rent Man called and made demands
Some mothers had no choice

"The Hill" Cumberland Street Market

My First Cousins, Angela and Paddy Kane

Story Fifty-Eight

I Took the Boat

I missed me darling mother

And I missed me father too

I even missed me Granny

But what else could I do?

I left me school at fourteen years

And couldn't get a job

I hung around the streets at night

I hadn't got a bob

I got in trouble with the Law

Now the judge was fair and kind

He said he'd give me sixteen months

If a job I couldn't find

It was there and then I decided

As I was putting on me coat

The only option left to me

Was to England and the boat.

The Da' he had a cousin

Who lived in Birmingham

He used to tell me stories

Of this kind and gentle man

And so he wrote a letter

And asked if he wouldn't mind

Taking me in for a month or two

To see if a job I could find

Now wait there and I'll tell yeah

It wasn't too easy at first

My Dublin accent didn't help

With a load of Culchies I was cursed

They knew the system inside out

And this Dub was fresh new meat

I worked from morning until dusk

My quota I had to meet.

Carrying bricks all over the site

I was filled with aches and pains

Pushing a barrow full of cement

Up the plank and down again

I'd crawl into me bed at night

Full of dust and grime

Longing for me Ma' and Da'

And the fun we'd have sometimes

But the strangest of things did happen

When I went to a dance one night

I was standing talking to me pals

When this Angel came in sight

With beautiful eyes of Emerald Green

And skin as soft as cream

With just one movement of her hand

She stepped out of my dream

Six months later we were wed

And the kids came fast and new

There was Paddy, James and Mary

And the last one we called Sue

I've tried me best with the chance I got

From the Judge in court that day

I tried to work hard all me life

And to train my kids that way

Story Fifty-Nine

Nobody's Child

My uncle told me stories from years ago about the poverty he witnessed while growing up in Dublin. He spoke of many families who struggled from day to day to feed their children and of the horrendous conditions in which they had to live. He said that it was no surprise for people living in tenement houses, in what we refer to today as the North Inner City, to find an abandoned baby left in their hallway or on the doorstep of a house in Elliott Place or Faithful Place. Many of these young children were abandoned in this area by people who lived elsewhere.

He said that there were many families in this area who never hesitated in taking in these little strays and giving them a home to live in with love and care and a place to lay their head. As a young boy he ran errands for many of the prostitutes from this area, he would clean and tidy their room whenever they were expecting a customer to call. He always spoke very kindly of these women, who did what they had to do, to feed their children and pay their rent.

I have based the following poem, on a particular story that he told me about, concerning one family in particular that lived beside his mother in Purdon Street in 1912.

My uncle told me that he had sailed around the world as a merchant seaman and had seen many countries where poverty was rife but that none of them was as bad as the area where he was born in Dublin City.

I was walking down the street that night

And I was all alone

Me Ma' she said she had no choice

But to leave me on my own

I never had a daddy to sit upon his knee

Me mammy left me standing there

Alone as I could be

I stood there in this doorway

As the rain came pelting down

My dress was soaked right to the skin

And my bare feet on the ground

I was standing there with me hair all drenched

When along came Misses Mac

Come here luv she said to me

With me you're coming back

To the little room I call me home

To a place you can lay your head

Sure there's plenty of room for the two of us

On the straw I call me bed'

This kindly woman named Misses Mac

Was an Angel from above

She taught me all that I should know

And showered me with her love

I'm all grown now and have my man

And children of my own

I tell them all of Misses Mac

And the love that I was shown

♦ ♦ ♦

Story Sixty

This photograph was taken by my uncle, Paddy Coffey (1905-1989). It was taken some time in the late 1930's. Paddy was home in Dublin on shore-leave and had brought home a new Box Camera that he'd bought on his travels abroad. On his return to his home area of the Monto he was surprised at how this area of Dublin had changed in the six months that he'd been away at sea.

A lot of the old tenement houses and Brothels were being demolished, side streets were swept away by bulldozers and old pubs were knocked down. And so, with his new camera he began photographing around his neighbourhood, family, friends, homes, old prostitutes and unwanted children who were claimed by families in the area. The young children in this photograph that he took were most probably orphaned children.

I was left behind a tenement door

One cold and weary night

Wrapped in a shawl

In a rain drenched hall

As my mother she took flight

The night wind howled up through the house

Like a Banshee at a Wake

Who cursed and cried

Like the Devil's Bride

For a child

Someone to take

No loving arms reached out to me

To comfort me from fright

No one could hear

My cries of fear

On that sad and dreary night

So I laid wrapped in my shawl

And my cries seemed all in vain

When the sweetest voice I've ever heard

Said "Hello, what's your name"

She gently took me in her arms

And held me to her breast

She turned around

And I heard her say

"Jem, I think we've just been blessed

With this little babe that no-one wants

We'll keep her for our own"

"Good on yeah Maggie" he replied

"We'll keep her till she's grown"

God sent two Angels from above

To bless my life with endless love

Other publications by this author

A Time of Innocence

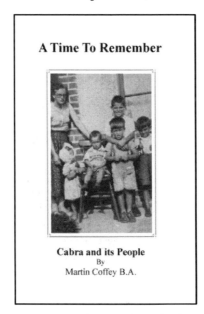

A Time to Remember

Tell Me A Story

My Neil Diamond Experience

Old Dublin Photos

I always tell the truth sometimes

Murder in the Monto

My Renehan Family History

The author was also involved in the following publications.

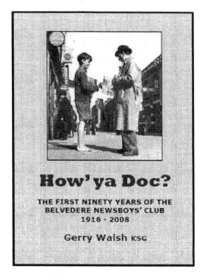

How' ya Doc?

Choosing the Positive